A Bright Ray
of Hope

A Bright Ray of Hope

THE PERPETUAL EDUCATION FUND

John K. Carmack

DESERET BOOK

SALT LAKE CITY, UTAH

To Shirley

Text and photographs on pages vi, 54, 62, 74, 106, 134, 154 © Intellectual Reserve, Inc. Used by permission.

Library of Congress Cataloging-in-Publication Data

Carmack, John K.
  A bright ray of hope : the Perpetual Education Fund / John K. Carmack.
    p. cm.
  Includes bibliographical references and index.
  ISBN 1-59038-234-X (hardcover : alk. paper)
  1. Perpetual Education Fund. 2. Mormon missionaries—Education.
I. Title.
  BX8661.C27 2004
  378.3'62'088289332—dc22

                                                2004014439

Printed in the United States of America   18961
R. R. Donnelley and Sons, Crawfordsville, IN

10   9   8   7   6   5   4   3   2   1

CONTENTS

MERIAM, PHILIPPINES

One of the first recipients of a PEF loan in the Philippines, Meriam was a shy returned missionary forced to provide for herself, her mother, and other family members. Inspired by a PEF fireside, she established a plan for her future, received a loan, and began a two-year program to become a Web designer.

She says: "The Lord has opened the door—I am so grateful—and I hope to repay my PEF loan before I graduate!"

INTRODUCTION

THREE YEARS HAD PASSED SINCE President Gordon B. Hinckley made an exciting announcment that the Church was establishing a new fund called the Perpetual Education Fund and creating a new department to administer the fund. Since then, more than 10,000 young adult Church members have received loans and career guidance, and many have graduated from vocational training that has given them a rich variety of practical skills designed to qualify them for better employment. Much had been accomplished in those three years, but those of us charged with establishing PEF wanted to hear directly the experiences and feelings of those young men and women who had been blessed by this initiative.

To learn more about these young people and also to train those charged with handling PEF in the field, Richard Cook and I went to Brazil. We chose Brazil because it was the country with the largest group of PEF recipients.

We arranged to meet with about eighty young people who had benefited from this program and who lived in or near Recife. We wanted to hear their stories and feel their spirit. We wanted to know about their dreams and goals, their experiences in school, their hopes for improving their economic circumstances, and their success in accomplishing their dreams and goals. We especially wanted to hear an expression of their feelings about PEF and the career guidance and loans that had been made available to them. This would give us some idea of whether we were on track in our efforts to carry out the grand vision and design announced by President Gordon B. Hinckley on 31 March 2001. In addition to completing a questionnaire, these young people shared their thoughts about and experiences with PEF in two lengthy sessions.

Those we interviewed glowed with the optimism and energy that we had hoped to find in them. They clearly represent the future of the Church in their own great country. I tried to scribble some of their words.

"PEF is an inspired program that helps me, my family, and people everywhere. It is the will of our Heavenly Father to help us." These words from the first to speak came from the young woman's heart. They typified the testimony each young person shared that PEF was inspired of the Lord.

The second one to speak continued the train of thought the first had started. "The PEF is a great blessing for me and my family. It has changed my family both spiritually and temporally." We had hoped and trusted that temporal blessings would accrue to the participants, but we had stressed that the greatest blessings would be spiritual. Young person after young person shared feelings about the dual effect PEF had had on their lives and on their families. It was hard to know where the temporal and spiritual blessings began and ended. The two kinds of blessings intertwined seamlessly, which should not have surprised us, given the Lord's declaration that all things in the gospel, including those seemingly temporal in nature, are spiritual.

The recipients continued, sharing their experiences. "I was unemployed for a time [after his mission]. I got my training and less than a week after graduating I was employed." Not everyone experienced such immediate success in finding a job, but many had, and almost all had gained skills that would eventually qualify them for gainful employment.

"I had no money for school, but with the PEF loan I can now study and make payments." All these young people understood that they had received a loan that must be repaid to help others receive similar blessings. Almost every person who had been helped came from an economically disadvantaged situation and because of their circumstances would have had little or no hope of receiving training and education. Their gratitude was deep, and they were quick to express it. First and foremost they were grateful to the Lord for inspiring the program. Next, and universally, they were grateful to President Hinckley and his associates for their love, interest, and vision. And finally, they were grateful to Church members and friends of the Church who had generously contributed to the fund.

"PEF is a light in the lives of every member of the Church." A bright ray of hope, indeed, had shined on people in need of help in obtaining education and training.

Some of their goals were as practical as those shared by one recipient who said: "My goal is to fix computers owned by Church members. I want to be the best computer repairman that ever was."

Speaking for many, another recipient said, "This is a blessing in our lives, given by Heavenly Father." Another added: "PEF is a miracle in my life. It came at exactly the right time." Several mentioned the timing of the program. There is, as Ecclesiastes declared so well, a time and a season for all things, and PEF seems to have been timed exactly right. As a result, as one said, "Now I have hope."

We have learned that young people from many lands had been praying for the kind of help PEF brought. For example, one said: "I asked the Lord what I could do, then PEF answered my prayers." Perhaps the young people of the Church prayed PEF into existence. One of them testified: "The Lord has given us this. We were prepared to receive it." This seems a true insight.

These eighty young people were energetic and absolutely glowed with optimism. We were thrilled when several ambitious sisters stepped confidently forward. Speaking for all of them, one said, "It [PEF] has brought a lot of self-esteem into my life." Self-esteem is vitally important in achieving successful lives, and PEF is bringing this blessing to thousands. If increasing self-esteem were all it did, PEF would be worth all the labor and resources expended in establishing it. We left Brazil with our own glowing optimism for the future of the Church in that important country.

We who were privileged to participate in the establishment and early growth of PEF have felt it important to document this global initiative, which is destined to bless the lives of tens and even hundreds of thousands of young adults. We hope members of the Church will find this story important, interesting, and inspiring. To that end we wish to share the history of this far-reaching program, cite some of the early successes, and leave a record of our thoughts about the purpose of PEF, its potential destiny, and the principles and doctrines that are at its foundation.

Most of us have a deep and sincere desire to help those who are deprived gain new hope and opportunities. This is especially true when we find young men and women with promise and ability thwarted in their efforts to improve their circumstances. One of the phrases we often hear and use in our prayers is: "Bless the poor and the needy, the sick and the afflicted, and those who have cause to mourn." Surely we should constantly pray for the poor and needy, but isn't there more to our duty toward others than merely dashing off that phrase? PEF has given Church members and others a real and practical way of helping young people raise themselves out of poverty into the light of a bright ray of new hope.

We may be superficially moved when we read about poverty in faraway places, but when we meet it face-to-face, we are stirred emotionally. My first memory of such an experience came about 1936. It was the time of the Great Depression, and poverty was widespread. I would have been five years old when a man dressed in tattered clothing came to our door in Winslow, Arizona, asking: "Could you spare some food and money? I am on the road, cold and hungry." The concern and empathy I felt on that occasion has never left me. As I remember, Mother then and always found something to spare for the poor and needy.

Unlike those who endured those bleak depression years, many

of us enjoy unprecedented abundance. Our homes have clean running water, indoor plumbing, ample space, and fine furnishings. We have ample supplies of food and clothing, to say nothing of the luxuries and conveniences we have largely come to take for granted. We can easily forget or ignore that a major percentage of the world's people lives in poverty, seriously lacking necessities. What can and should we with plenty do to help those living in poverty? Can the Church, now a worldwide institution, find ways to help without weakening its members? Is administering to the needs of the poor merely a good thing to do or an imperative duty?

Those of us responsible for establishing the Perpetual Education Fund of The Church of Jesus Christ of Latter-day Saints have been privileged participants in a work directed from above, through the vision and foresight of President Gordon B. Hinckley and his associates in the First Presidency and the Quorum of Twelve Apostles. Much has come to pass in this initiative since its announcement in the 171st annual general conference, on 31 March 2001. To see the light of hope enter the eyes of ambitious young men and women when they discover a way to reach goals that previously seemed unattainable has been a high privilege indeed. We desire to share this experience and joy with others.

Our task has been to help the Church achieve the divine purposes of the modern PEF, patterned after the nineteenth century Perpetual Emigrating Fund. The principles of the program are the doctrines and principles of the gospel. Everywhere we have gone, we have felt keen interest in and heartfelt support for PEF. The strong interest and desire to know more about it compelled us to put our hand to the task of sharing the experience. As President Hinckley has said on a number of occasions, it has been a miracle. Only future events will reveal its full impact and spiritual purposes, but sharing its beginning may make a small contribution to that understanding.

Our leader and spokesman has been President Gordon B. Hinckley, and we rely primarily on his public announcements and explanations of PEF, while sharing our own experiences and thoughts about it.

What we have written and share here includes an explanation of what those of us, charged with the practical tasks of bringing to fruition the announced purposes of PEF, have done and experienced. We also share our thoughts of gospel meanings behind the events. The book can serve as a case study in how gospel principles can bring about practical changes for less-advantaged young people in the Church. With many people working together under the direction of the prophet, we have been able to marshal the machinery and voluntary contributions of members of the Church to meet a real need. The book may be of interest also to a broader segment of readers interested in the subject of helping young men and women rise out of poverty by gaining marketable skills. Contributors, large and small, will naturally and understandably find interest in learning what the Church has done with money they have generously donated. Our hope is that this book will satisfy these and other reasonable desires.

This is a story that has a definite beginning but will never have an end. We see its benefits expanding in ever-widening circles, like ripples on a body of water. The PEF story begins with the problem of crushing poverty. The problem is a global one, not a narrow or isolated circumstance. Deprivation is the seedbed of not only economic but sociological problems, affecting not just the billions who suffer directly but all of us. Meeting these problems required vision and leadership, which was provided by President Hinckley. His inspired solution is rooted in the teachings of the Savior and is not without historical precedence in the Church. It incorporates a contemporary application of a proven pattern for helping needy individuals and families.

The generosity of thousands of Church members has brought to reality the vision of PEF. President Hinckley's description of the need and the solution was so articulate that its feasibility became immediately apparent to those who heard it. Genius and inspiration often seem simple and right, especially when coming from the lips of a prophet. It seems obvious now that education is the answer to the question of poverty. What was not so obvious was how to finance that education and training for those who can't afford it. Some of the governing principles had already been revealed in the welfare program of the Church—self-reliance, spirituality, and individual responsibility. But there remained unanswered questions, such as: From where will the resources come? How will the process be administered? Who will undertake such a global task? Under President Hinckley's inspired direction, these are some of the issues and questions we have grappled with during the early phases of this work.

When charged with the responsibility of implementing PEF, I needed immediate help. As will be shown, Chad Evans and Rex Allen came to my rescue. They worked tirelessly to help create the department and the machinery that administers this program. Just when we needed someone with global financial experience, Elder

Richard Cook completed his service in the Second Quorum of Seventy. He agreed to join our volunteer team as director of finance. As the loan applications began pouring in, an energetic, experienced, and hardworking couple, Elder Gordon and Sister Janice Creer, joined our team. They rolled up their sleeves and accepted every challenge to make this work. As the Brethren delegated to our department other related programs to administer and problems to solve, we found Elder Ronald and Sister Afton Ririe, who had the background and experience necessary to answer this need. Others, including Brent Plowman and Kenneth Raines, representing the Church's professional accounting and financial control team, brought stability and control to the processes. Subsequently Brad Jacox, who was our second controller, and Tom Rueckert, who followed him, made huge contributions in meeting our accounting challenges. The Church allowed us one secretary. Debbie Muir has been that person, and she has helped us with virtually all of our duties. The PEF board of directors, chaired by President Gordon B. Hinckley, has guided us every step of the way.

Hundreds of others, from nearly every department of Church administration, have given generously of their time, talents, inspiration, and support. Thousands have made it work in the field. In all that we have done, the Church Educational System (CES) has been our partner under the watchful eye of the Church Commissioner of Education, Elder Henry B. Eyring of the Quorum of Twelve Apostles. Paul V. Johnson (and before him, Stanley A. Peterson), administrator of seminaries, institutes, and Church schools, has given direct and loyal support. The service rendered by Roger Christensen, secretary to the Church Board of

Education and the man responsible for the CES finances, has been invaluable. Institute directors and their leaders in the parts of the world impacted by PEF have been there, working directly with the young people. Priesthood leaders out in the field, including the bishoprics, stake presidencies, and area presidencies of the participants, have helped keep this program on a spiritual plane. We have also forged a most important partnership with employment resource centers, area controllers, directors of temporal affairs, and many others. We desire to give credit where it is due, without being able to go beyond naming these few names.

The following is the story of PEF to this point. It is not an official document of The Church of Jesus Christ of Latter-day Saints. Because it is written from my own perspective, I take sole responsibility for it and for any errors that exist. On behalf of all who have been involved, I give thanks to our Savior and Redeemer for the privilege of serving those who have been and are being lifted from the darkness of disadvantage, poverty, and hopelessness. May the success of PEF be an inspiration to everyone who reads these pages, particularly to the hundreds of thousands of generous donors who have created the fund.

CHAPTER ONE

WE HAVE A PROBLEM

The people that walked in darkness
have seen a great light: they that dwell in the
land of the shadow of death, upon them
hath the light shined.

ISAIAH 9:2

A FEELING OF HUSHED EXPECTANCY fell over the enormous congregation of priesthood holders gathered in the gleaming new
Conference Center on the evening of 31 March 2001. Twenty-one
thousand men and boys filled the cavernous meeting hall, gathered to share their common brotherhood, hear their leaders
expound the gospel, and gain a greater vision of Church government and priesthood responsibilities. Through a satellite system,
similar congregations all over the world were connected by sight
and sound to the Salt Lake City General Priesthood Meeting,
making this truly a worldwide gathering of male members of the
Church.

Several leaders had already spoken, including members of the
First Presidency, Presidents James E. Faust and Thomas S.
Monson. As the two-hour meeting reached its climax, every ear
and heart listened intently as President Gordon B. Hinckley

stepped to a pulpit fabricated with wood from a tree he himself had once planted in his yard. Immaculately dressed and groomed and filled with energy, enthusiasm, and vision, he seemed years younger than his true age of 90 as he focused undimmed eyes on the vast seen and unseen congregation. His usual ready wit, friendly smile, and avuncular manner was now replaced by a completely serious demeanor. Delivered in simple, direct, and powerful English and translated into scores of languages, his message was impossible to misunderstand. The members of the Church had for many years recognized his extraordinary wisdom, gained in a lifetime of service to the Church, the community, and the world. But now and for the previous six years, he was speaking as *the* prophet, seer, and revelator—the one man on earth ordained and sustained to lead the worldwide Church, declare the word of God, and hold all of the earthly keys of the priesthood. His was the right and solemn obligation to guide, as had Moses, the whole congregation of Israel.

His leadership over those six years had been dynamic, even beyond the expectation of Church members accustomed to his forceful and forward-looking leadership. The Latter-day Saints had come to anticipate his announcement of new initiatives and programs of great interest and import as he addressed them, especially in the priesthood session, but few were prepared for what followed that evening.

As one steeped in the rich history of the rise and progress of the Church, President Hinckley began as he often did with a reference to an historical event, explaining a problem that Church leaders faced under Brigham Young's leadership in 1849. The monumental problem they then wrestled with was how to bring to the Intermountain valleys the converts who by the thousands were uniting themselves with the Church in Great Britain, Scandinavia, and other parts of Europe—the fruits of the dynamic missionary program the Prophet Joseph Smith had launched two decades earlier. It seemed likely that these converts would number in the tens of thousands. And new converts almost all wanted to gather with the main body of the Saints in Utah. Most of these early members were of modest means, many owning little or nothing of this world's goods. What could be done to help finance their emigration to America and meet the expense of outfitting them to travel to the Salt Lake Valley?

Brigham Young, the prophet at that time, had the inspired answer. The Saints, most of them poor themselves, would contribute money and in-kind property to a new and separate Church fund called the Perpetual Emigrating Fund, known to Latter-day Saints as the PEF. From this fund those of limited means could borrow enough money to allow them to come to Utah with their families. After they became established, it was understood they would repay their loans as best they could, thereby replenishing the fund and enabling others to enjoy the same privilege. Thus was the descriptive adjective *perpetual* placed in the name of the fund.

President Hinckley's historic reference caught the immediate attention of his listeners, most of whom were at least vaguely aware of Church history and the courage, sacrifice, and valor of the Mormon pioneers. But where was President Hinckley taking them with this reference to Church history?

Quickly the prophet switched to the present-day Church and a current need:

"We have many missionaries, both young men and young women, who are called locally and who serve with honor in Mexico, Central America, South America, the Philippines, and other places. They have very little money, but they make a contribution with what they have. They are largely supported from the General Missionary Fund to which many of you contribute. . . . They become excellent missionaries working side by side with elders and sisters sent from the United States and Canada. While in this service they come to know how the Church operates. . . . Then comes the day of their release. They return to their homes. Their hopes are high. But many of them have great difficulty finding employment because they have no skills. They sink right back into the pit of poverty from which they came."[1]

He then outlined the cycle of poverty that these missionaries face when they return home. Crediting the inspiration of the Lord for its conception, President Hinckley came quickly to the point by outlining and proposing a plan to establish a fund from voluntary contributions by Church members. The earnings of the fund would be used to make loans to deserving and determined young men and women, "for the most part returned missionaries."[2] The principles underlying the use of the fund would be based on "similar principles to those underlying the Perpetual Emigration Fund."[3]

Then, in a manner that linked the new with the old, he named the new fund the Perpetual Education Fund. The initials that would come to be known among the Saints were the same as the historical PEF. The recipients of the loans would be young people who had served the Lord and needed help in gaining an education or vocational skills that would permit them to seek better employment. The prophet went on.

"It is expected that they will attend school in their own communities. They can live at home. We have an excellent institute program established in these countries where they can be kept close to the Church. The directors of these institutes are familiar with the educational opportunities in their own cities. Initially, most of these students will attend technical schools where they will learn such things as computer science, refrigeration engineering, and other skills that are in demand and for which they can become qualified. The plan may later be extended to training for the professions."[4]

He further explained that the Church expected those young people to attend institute and that the institute director would keep track of their progress.

"Those desiring to participate in the program will make application to the institute director. He will clear them through their local bishops and stake presidents to determine that they are worthy and in need of help. Their names and the prescribed amount of their loans will then be sent to Salt Lake City, where funds will be issued, payable not to the individual but to the institution where they will receive their schooling."[5]

As we see, President Hinckley spelled out the program in significant detail. He explained that the young people would be expected to repay the loans, with a small amount of interest, thus helping others who would later need the same kind of help.

He continued: "We shall have a strong oversight board here in Salt Lake and a director of the program who will be an emeritus General Authority, a man with demonstrated business and technical skills and who has agreed to accept this responsibility as a volunteer."[6] The announcement touched the congregation of men and boys. Many wept openly, and with their tears came a desire on the part of many to become involved in some meaningful way, certainly to become contributors to the fund. The prophet had provided a simple and powerful new opportunity to contribute to a process designed to assist others in less-advantaged circumstances. The modern PEF, like its historic counterpart, provided an opportunity that virtually everyone could participate in. The Conference Center was alive with excitement.

The prophet suggested that they would begin that fall, in the year 2001, on a modest basis, but added: "We can envision the time when this program will benefit a very substantial number."[7] He next shared his vision of the good that could come of the program.

"With good employment skills, these young men and women can rise out of the poverty they and generations before them have known. They will better provide for their families. They will serve in the Church and grow in leadership and responsibility. They will repay their loans to make it possible for others to be blessed as they have been blessed. It will become a revolving fund. As faithful members of the Church, they will pay their tithes and offerings, and the Church will be much the stronger for their presence in the areas where they live."[8]

What a breathtaking vision! The scope of this initiative was mind-boggling, and the prophet announced it to the whole Church. His faith in it was clear.

"Now, this is a bold initiative, but we believe in the need for it and in the success that it will enjoy. It will be carried forward as an official program of the Church with all that this implies. It will become a blessing to all whose lives it touches—to the young men and women, to their future families, to the Church that will be blessed with their strong local leadership."[9]

Stressing the principle of self-reliance through repayment of the loans, President Hinckley expressed his confidence in the future recipients of the loans.

"The beneficiaries will repay the money, and when they do so, they will enjoy a wonderful sense of freedom because they have improved their lives not through a grant or gift, but through borrowing and then repaying. They can hold their heads high in a spirit of independence. The likelihood of their remaining faithful and active throughout their lives will be very high."[10]

He then discussed the great initiatives in employment services going forward under the welfare program of the Church. He differentiated PEF from the employment program. "The matter of education will rest with the Perpetual Education Fund. The one is a rotating education fund to make possible the development of skills. The other is the placing of men and women in improved employment who already have some marketable skills."[11]

We shall see that the two programs go hand in hand, each helping the other achieve its assigned role. By making it a separate, though related, enterprise of education, and by tying it in with the old PEF, President Hinckley created a winning metaphor for the program. Church members who heard the talk or read about it were stunned and thrilled. Tears flowed openly, and many of the Saints received an instant confirmation of the divine source of the dramatic announcement. A prophet of God had spoken and announced what might be called the spiritual creation of a whole new initiative to meet one of the great current concerns of the Brethren.

President Hinckley continued, expressing the thought and the desire that this program be carried out within the existing organization of the Church, with mostly volunteers doing the work, starting with the managing director. We shall see that this thought was basically carried out, but the vast global scope of PEF required deployment of resources and leaders into uncharted waters. For example, the institutes of religion of the Church had to shoulder new responsibilities affecting the temporal salvation of the young people entrusted to their care, where hitherto they had been mostly concerned with adding to the spiritual knowledge and commitment of young people preparing for life through education. The time that would be required to manage this new initiative was significant and would add to institute administrators' burdens, supplanting as well as augmenting other great spiritual responsibilities.

PEF would also impact virtually every Church department and function, including: accounting, controlling, financial, treasury, priesthood, fund raising, information management, welfare, auditing, public affairs, and investing. Church headquarters would need to allocate resources and focus its ingenuity on implementing this bold initiative, or what we might term its physical creation. In the field, many Church leaders, including bishops, stake presidents, institute leaders, area presidencies, controllers, employment and welfare workers, clerks, Church Educational System administrators, and volunteers would need to help in the work. PEF would change the landscape of the Church in areas where it was implemented. If Church leaders all over the world had not accepted it as a prophet-directed and heaven-inspired program, PEF could never have gotten off the ground but would have merely been a visionary idea without a practical future.

President Hinckley invited people to invest voluntarily in PEF. He explained that the Church had already received some substantial donations, but the corpus would need to grow to achieve the vast purposes of PEF. He suggested: "We will need considerably more. We invite others who wish to contribute to do so."[12] We shall see that the members, and in some cases friends of the Church, took his suggestion to heart. Donations immediately began to arrive in wards, branches, and at Church headquarters. A special line was added to the Church donation slip, and PEF, as a fund created by donations, became an instant reality. A way had been opened for the Saints to help young adults around the Church, who desperately needed hope and a little help in the form of a loan.

As he closed his address, President Hinckley said:

"I believe the Lord does not wish to see his people condemned to live in poverty. I believe he would have the faithful enjoy the good things of the earth. He would have us do these things to help them. And he will bless us as we do so. For the success of this undertaking I humbly pray, while soliciting your interest, your faith, your prayers, your concerns in its behalf."[13]

As President Hinckley concluded and took his seat in the Conference Center, a nearly universal reaction to the declaration occurred at once. Almost all who heard, and later those who read about the announcement, felt they had been privileged to witnesses a great new revelation pronounced and spelled out in detail, simplicity, and power. Many of those working and living abroad, including an increasing number of Church members, have been deeply moved by widespread poverty. Church members, as a natural reaction to what they have witnessed, have desired to help those living and serving in poverty and hopelessness.

The Church had been providing aid to countries needing assistance, especially in response to natural disasters such as floods, hurricanes, earthquakes, and drought. Contributions making possible such help poured into the Church, and the Church had established a department and charitable foundation called LDS Charities that uses those funds carefully and liberally to aid victims at home and abroad, in and out of the Church.

Still, meeting emergencies was not enough. Something more fundamental and long-lasting was needed, something that would strike at the core causes of poverty. That something was needed on a global scale. Now a major new call to join the prophet in a bold new initiative made it possible for the Saints to participate in an effort to help our young people better themselves. And join they did, by the hundreds of thousands.

The Church's missionary program for young men and women is an amazing and powerful success story that has sparked the interest of people and churches worldwide. During the early days of the Church, in simpler times, men such as Parley P. Pratt, on joining the Church through baptism, immediately dropped what they were doing, and without formal calls began missions to share the gospel. As the Church grew, the Church formalized those missions and organized the Saints into an effective missionary force. Members of the Quorum of the Twelve were often on missions at home and abroad. It was largely their work in Great Britain that brought about the need for the first PEF.

Even during the early part of the 20th century, only those who lived in the intermountain area had the opportunity to serve full-time missions. But Church policy gradually changed to allow members to serve as missionaries regardless of where they lived. Then came the true internationalization of the Church as a world-wide institution beginning approximately with the era presided over by President David O. McKay. The rapid growth of the Church in such places as Mexico, Central America, South America, and the Philippines brought thousands and thousands into full-time missionary service from those countries. Many of these missionaries and their families, unlike those from the United States, Canada, Great Britain, and other industrialized nations, had only meager resources to handle the expense of serving a mission. Nor was the early practice of living off the generosity of the people—serving without purse or scrip—a practical or acceptable solution in the increasingly urban societies of the world.

These conditions brought about the creation of the General Missionary Fund, to which Church members were invited to contribute. This fund enabled men and women in less affluent countries to serve missions. This expanded greatly the number of young men and women who could serve the Lord in the mission fields of the Church. Serving a mission was an honor now available to those in outlying and poor areas where the Church was growing. Of course these young people and their families paid as much of their own expenses as possible, but most of them received much of their support from the General Missionary Fund.

Gaining opportunities through the General Missionary Fund created problems of adjustment for some missionaries following their releases. These missionaries had learned how to dress according to missionary standards, which were higher than most had ever dreamed of adopting. They had lived on equal financial footing with their missionary companions and associates from more developed countries. All of this prepared them to provide leadership and service after their missions, but it also exposed them to a relatively affluent lifestyle such as they had never previously known. Returning home, the reality of their situation often brought a rude awakening. Their bright hope turned bleak. Their ambition to improve themselves sometimes turned to ashes. Hopelessness replaced hope. Discouragement replaced optimism.

Using skills learned in the mission field and drawing upon their native intelligence and talents, some found their way despite these discouraging obstacles. Their companions from less disadvantaged backgrounds had often found them equal to and more able than themselves, but after returning home and losing the support they had received during their missions, these impoverished young men and women faced a hard reality—the crushing poverty out of which they had been delivered only temporarily. The mission itself had provided some tremendous benefits: an education in language, true empathy for people, a desire to help, and the ability to speak, write, and converse effectively. Still, they needed something more. What should it be?

Wanting to help, many returning missionaries from affluent circumstances tried what seemed natural and humane. They and their families would often provide the means for their former companions to come to the United States where education and training were readily available. It became apparent, however, that many—perhaps most—of those afforded this opportunity did not return to their countries where their service and education could be used to build up the Church and improve their communities. Those who weren't able to call upon former missionary companions for assistance, came to depend on friends in their own home wards, branches, stakes, and missions, who did what they could to help these returned missionaries. But local resources were generally limited.

By the time President Hinckley announced the formation of the PEF in 2001, thousands of missionaries were completing missions annually in countries such as Mexico, Brazil, Chile, the Philippines, Peru, Argentina, Guatemala, and Africa. These young people often had to accept menial work that paid scarcely enough for them to subsist. Even marriage and family were hard to consider. Clearly there existed a severe and growing problem. While many courageously went forward and found ways to improve themselves, something more was needed.

Because the Brethren constantly travel and tour missions, attending stake and regional conferences, they knew that the problems described here existed and were worsening. Surely the local leaders shared many ideas and expressed themselves about how to meet and solve these problems. The Church councils appointed committees to study the problem, and these committees completed reports and made recommendations. The ideas were many and varied, and the recommendations often specific and well-considered. But the need persisted and grew. It was something that weighed heavily on the minds and in the hearts of the First Presidency, the Twelve, the Seventy, the Presiding Bishopric, and the general leaders of the auxiliaries. Church leaders all over the world sent suggestions and information on conditions.

Every area of the Church made regular formal reports to the

General Authorities and to the Area Committee, a committee charged with coordinating the work in all the areas of the Church. The Church had the equivalent of its own state department in the work of the Area Committee. The amount of information available was massive and detailed. This information supported the conclusion that we had a problem that was persistent and growing.

This brought us to 31 March 2001, and the prophet's declaration that the Church would establish the Perpetual Education Fund. Church members, now keenly interested and aware of the new initiative, awaited further word from the Brethren. The announcement had been made; the time had come for intense planning and vigorous execution.

NOTES

1. Gordon B. Hinckley, in Conference Report, 31 March 2001, 67.
2. Ibid., 68.
3. Ibid., 67.
4. Ibid., 68.
5. Ibid.
6. Ibid.
7. Ibid.
8. Ibid.
9. Ibid.
10. Ibid., 68–69.
11. Ibid., 69.
12. Ibid.
13. Ibid., 69–70.

CHAPTER TWO

A PATTERN OF CARING

We covenant "never to cease our
exertions until all the Saints who desire, should
be removed to a place of safety."

BRIGHAM YOUNG, NAUVOO, 1846

IN AN EARLY REVELATION THE Lord told Joseph Smith that He does "not walk in crooked paths, neither doth he turn to the right hand nor to the left, neither doth he vary from that which he hath said, therefore his paths are straight, and *his course is one eternal round*" (D&C 3:2; emphasis added). How does a seemingly new program, announced to the Church by President Hinckley, fit into the gospel plan? And how does its course fit into the history of the restored Church of our Savior?

Since PEF is founded on gospel principles, it would not likely take the Church away from its past in a startlingly new direction, but rather would fit well with Church history. Surely it would be based on everlasting principles designed to meet current challenges. Its foundation would be discernible in times past, the present time, and likely will be seen to meet conditions in times to come. We shall demonstrate that PEF is indeed a most effective approach to a current problem, based on a continuum of past applications of eternal principles to major problems faced by our people. If this is so, what were those problems, and how did our leaders meet them?

Serving daily as the managing director of PEF, my tongue has slipped a number of times in calling the Perpetual Education Fund the Perpetual Emigrating Fund. Given the similarity of not only the names but the aims of the two programs, this shouldn't be surprising. I have had an ongoing feeling that in a sense, we are just continuing the work Brigham Young initiated with the Perpetual Emigrating Fund.

Throughout its history, the Church has addressed the problems of poor and less-advantaged members. Indeed, the Lord has so commanded us. "And remember in all things the poor and the needy, the sick and the afflicted, for he that doeth not these things, the same is not my disciple" (D&C 52:40). The governing principles of this program are traceable throughout this dispensation. How Church leaders have met problems of the poor in the past, by applying simple and powerful principles, is a fascinating story. Let's begin.

With Joseph Smith in jail during the dark days of Missouri, leadership of necessity devolved upon Brigham Young and the Quorum of the Twelve. The Prophet Joseph had lodged authoritative priesthood keys with the Twelve, and Brigham Young was the President of the Twelve. Facing an extermination order, Church members had to leave Missouri or risk annihilation. On the shoulders of President Young rested that difficult leadership responsibility. The Brethren met to plan the exodus from Missouri to

Illinois. During the meeting, President Young introduced this powerful motion:

"Resolved that we this day enter into a covenant to stand by and assist each other to the utmost of our abilities in removing from this state, and that we will never desert the poor who are worthy, till they shall be out of the reach of the exterminating order of General Clark, acting for and in the name of the state."[1]

This motion duly carried and became the guiding principle of President Young's leadership. In a sense the covenant those leaders made was a forerunner of the modern-day PEF.

A few years later, after the slaying of Joseph and Hyrum Smith in Carthage Jail, Brigham Young became the leader of the Church. Circumstances forced the Twelve, under the leadership of President Young, to find a new place for the Saints to settle. They hastened to complete the temple they had been constructing in Nauvoo, so that fleeing families could be armed with the spirituality, inspiration, and protection afforded by the temple ordinances. Thousands of Saints then prepared to leave their beautiful city and new temple behind, and head west to a new home. Many were so poor that they had insufficient means to acquire the wagons, food, and the provisions necessary for the long, arduous journey. Their leaders met in the Nauvoo Temple to lay plans for undertaking the exodus.

Elder George A. Smith of the Twelve, a cousin of Joseph Smith, reminded the Brethren assembled in the temple that during the dark Missouri era, their leaders had entered into a covenant to bring all of the poor to safety. He suggested it was time to make a similar covenant. President Young put the proposal in the form of a motion "that we take all the saints with us, to the extent of our ability, that is, our influence and property."[2] The motion carried unanimously, whereupon President Young prophesied that God would bless them with the means to accomplish the resolution. We can't help but remember President Hinckley's announcement of the establishment of PEF in the 171st annual general conference and his prediction that the Lord would prosper the vast new global initiative. In creating the Perpetual Education Fund, he was continuing the course followed by the Lord's people, drawing on the experience and principles that had brought the Saints to the point they now are and inviting all who desired to help to contribute.

In the only revelation recorded in the Doctrine and Covenants that came through President Brigham Young, the Lord revealed the basic organization for the exodus to the West. The revelation included directions for taking care of the poor.

"Let each company bear an equal proportion, according to the dividend of their property, in taking the poor, the widows, the fatherless, and the families of those who have gone into the army [the Mormon Battalion], that the cries of the widow and the fatherless come not up into the ears of the Lord against this people" (D&C 136:8).

This placed a divine imprimatur on the covenant to care for the poor in the exodus west. The Saints were true to this covenant.

Once the Saints had settled in the West, they faced a new problem. The leaders' solution to it inaugurated the next step in the continuing covenant to remember the needs of the poor. In 1849, the Church began to establish a fund to help the growing number of converts in Europe come to the Great Salt Lake Valley. Many found the means to come without financial help, but the very poor could not. The Church needed a major program with resources and organization to back it up.

Under the inspiration and direction of President Young, Church leaders inaugurated a bold plan for assisting emigrants from Europe in their desire to gather to Zion. Facing the complexities of gathering funds, making loans, and administering a program of immigration on an intercontinental scale, Church leaders decided to establish a corporation to administer the whole process under the umbrella of the provisional State of Deseret. On 14 September 1850, the general assembly of the State of Deseret met in the Bowery in Great Salt Lake City. In that meeting, Church leaders introduced "an ordinance incorporating the Perpetual Emigrating Company." The general assembly discussed, amended, and passed the ordinance. The Articles of Incorporation conferred on the Perpetual Emigrating Company the usual powers of a corporation to act. The articles established a leadership team of not less than thirteen men to administer its affairs. One of the designated leaders was to be named president and the others assistants. The articles also designated a secretary, treasurer, and recorder to conduct the business of the corporation.

On the next day, the Church held a public meeting at the Bowery. As he had done in the Nauvoo Temple, Elder George A. Smith spoke in behalf of the poor. He reminded those present that Church members had entered into a covenant "not to cease their exertions until every Saint who wished to go was removed, which was done."[3] President Young called to the attention of the conference the organization of the new Perpetual Emigrating Company. He said: "It is now in a shape that makes it comprehensible; we have the legal right, from the authorities of the State, to pursue

lawfully, a system to gather the Poor."⁴ Upon motion duly presented and unanimously carried, the conference elected Brigham
Young president of the Perpetual Emigrating Company. He then
nominated eighteen prominent men as assistants, and those
assembled duly elected them.

That evening, at another meeting convened to complete the
organization of the corporation, those assembled elected Newel K.
Whitney as treasurer, Thomas Bullock as recorder, Willard
Richards as secretary, and John Brown and Orson Hyde as
traveling agents. They also made other appointments to perform
work in the various parts of the Church, such as visiting the members to collect donations. On 26 September 1850, the corporation
nominated Franklin D. Richards and Orson Pratt to be agents for
the company in England. The corporation immediately began to
function and fulfill its purposes. The fund administered by the
corporation consisted of some cash, but also included cattle and
other in-kind donations.

At a later meeting of the officers, President Young explained
that the corporation's property and funds were distinct from
Church tithing. The property was to be preserved "for the purpose
it was intended and should be preserved sacred but it shall not be
used for any poor person who is gathered to this Valley; let them
work for their own living."⁵

Now the immense migration from Europe to the American
West began. The Church had begun doing missionary work in
England by 1837. By 1841, the Church had made 6,614 converts,
and in the next ten years that number increased to 32,894. In
addition, many Church converts in Scandinavia were also awaiting emigration. In 1852, President Young sent this word to

Church members in Europe: "When a people, or individuals, hear the Gospel, obey its first principles, are baptized for the remission of their sins, and receive the Holy Ghost by the laying on of hands, it is time for them to gather, without delay, to Zion."[6] This applied to the Saints in Great Britain, Scandinavia, and Germany.

The First Presidency also directed them to gather diligently, warning that "he who has an opportunity to gather, and does not improve it, will be afflicted by the devil."[7]

PEF leaders designed principles of self-reliance for the program. They admonished the Saints to "help themselves to the utmost of their ability."[8] Agents organized three types of emigrating companies. The first included those who could pay all of their expenses; the second, those who could pay part of their expenses, but needed a loan for the balance; and the third, the poor who could not pay anything. Those receiving PEF loans signed notes to be repaid at a later date, after they became settled and had the means to pay. Historians vary in estimating how many came to Salt Lake Valley with the help of PEF, but it is probable that about 100,000 Saints were assisted. Many of them paid their own way, but the side benefit of the loan program was that a tremendous organization benefited all who came, whether they borrowed money for their expenses or used their own resources. Thus PEF became a catalyst that affected almost every aspect of the Church.

In 1853, 2,312 immigrated to Utah from Europe. About 955 paid their own way, about 1,000 received partial assistance, and only 400 needed loans for virtually all of their expenses.[9] When we consider that the Church membership in the Salt Lake Valley numbered approximately 6,000 in 1849, we gain some perspective of how important this program was in laying the foundation for the Church as we know it today. All who came were aided in some way by the organization of the PEF Corporation with its agents stationed at critical points along the way to render assistance.

These agents did the pick and shovel work of getting the Saints to the Salt Lake Valley. Agents labored in England, Scandinavia, and at key points of arrival in the United States. As one historian observed: "The Mormon emigrant . . . found himself escorted by men he knew, in the company of fellow converts, and with the assurance of a welcome which would direct his settlement at journey's end. Every detail of outfitting, lodging, feeding, and transporting was prearranged."[10] Using cooperative buying power to reduce costs, agents in the United States purchased wagons and provisions for companies and organized their arduous journeys. In 1853, the food allowance for a company of ten crossing the plains was 1,000 pounds of flour, 50 of sugar, 50 of bacon, 50 of rice, 30 of beans, 25 of salt, 20 of dried apples and peaches, 5 of tea, 1 jar of vinegar and 10 bars of soap.[11] (A journey across the plains usually took about 80 days.) Later President Young sent relief wagons from Salt Lake to meet incoming parties and acquired Fort Bridger and Fort Supply in Wyoming as stations to assist the wagon trains and handcart companies. Many members of the Church have forebears who came to Zion with the aid of this system.

In England or Scandinavia, PEF agents would charter a ship to carry the emigrants when they had enough applicants. They would notify the passengers by sending out circular announcements containing details of the journey. Emigrants would find a way to Liverpool and go immediately on board the chartered ships. Often a ship would have as many as a thousand emigrants. Leaders would appoint a president who would choose two counselors to preside on the journey. Leaders would divide the emigrants into wards or branches, each with a bishop or branch president to preside.

The famous English author Charles Dickens boarded one such emigrant ship, the *Amazon,* to report what he observed. He published this account:

"Two or three Mormon agents stood ready to hand them on to the Inspector, and to hand them forward when they had passed. By what successful means, a special aptitude for organization had been infused into these people I am, of course, unable to report. But I know that even now, there was no disorder, hurry, or difficulty. . . . I went on board their ship to bear testimony against them if they deserved it, as I fully believed they would; to my great astonishment they did not deserve it; and my predispositions and tendencies must not affect me as an honest witness. I went over the Amazon's side, feeling it impossible to deny that so far, some remarkable influence had produced a remarkable result, which better known influences have often missed."[12]

President Young gave precedence to people who had special skills and could help build communities. He made no secret of his desire to receive iron manufacturers, metal workers, textile manufacturers, potters, woodworkers, and other skilled and trained men and women. He asked the agents and leaders to search out people with these kinds of abilities and to "emigrate them in preference to anyone else."[13] Between 1850 and 1854, for example, they brought over boot and shoemakers, accountants, boilermakers, cabinetmakers, engineers, miners, masons, printers, spinners, weavers,

and many others representing specialized skills and occupations.[14]
We shall demonstrate later how closely the thinking of the leaders
in that day parallels our current leaders' direction.

When the emigrants arrived in Salt Lake City, an assignment
committee arranged celebrations with melons, cakes, dancing,
singing, and a rousing welcome with the firing of a cannon when
they passed Temple Square. The committee also readied settlement
locations to receive the new arrivals.

After the emigrants settled, the PEF enlisted the help of bishops and others to assist in loan collection. Many repaid their loans
in-kind or by laboring on Church and community projects, cash
being hard to acquire. When emigrants were slow in making payments, President Young got on their cases. He would remind them
of their obligations during his addresses to the Saints. For
example, when the indebtedness reached $56,000, he said: "I want
you to understand fully that I intend to put the screws upon
you."[15]

Keeping the fund solvent required diligence and ingenuity.
Donations came from many sources and were often in-kind. For
instance, wards and communities established the "Moroni Fund,"
the "Ephraim Fund," and the "Provo Fund." The Scandinavian
Choir in Salt Lake City held benefit concerts to raise money for
the fund. In Ephraim, Sarah Ann Peterson, the Relief Society
president, urged the sisters to donate all eggs laid on Sunday.
Other settlements followed suit. Some swore that the chickens laid
more eggs on Sunday than on any other day.[16] To keep the fund
alive and sufficient, the Church contributed tithing to the fund.

Block teachers, bishops, and tithing offices helped in collecting contributions. President Young and other Church leaders were

personally generous. President Young sold one of his homes and donated the proceeds to the fund. In commenting on the need to be generous, he observed from personal experience: "There is a giving that enriches."[17]

In meeting commitments to a certain number of emigrants each year, the fund was sometimes overextended and had to resort to a bank draft to pay the expenses of companies of emigrants. When PEF was short of cash to repay banks, merchants, cattle dealers, and others, President Young would tell the lenders something akin to the following (taken from an 1855 sermon): "I will pay you when I can, and not before. . . . It is the poor who have got your money, and if you have any complaints to make, make them against the Almighty for having so many poor."[18]

In 1852, Elder Erastus Snow cautioned members in Copenhagen, Denmark, that no one had a special right to use the funds, but that "every brother, sister, or family might with diligence and economy strive to help themselves and by a Saintly walk make themselves worthy to receive assistance. . . ."[19]

The work of PEF required much energy and planning by the Saints. Christian Madsen's letter to John Van Cott in 1861 captures the intensity of feeling and dedication as well. "Everywhere among the Saints the next year's emigration is almost their every thought. This circumscribes their prayers, their anxieties, and their exertions."[20] But the end was near for this great program.

After President Young's death, Church members sustained President John Taylor as President of the Church. Horace S. Eldredge had replaced President Young as president of the Perpetual Emigrating Company when President Young resigned in 1870. In 1873, Albert Carrington succeeded Eldredge. John

Taylor designated the year 1880 as a Jubilee Year in order to cele-
brate the 50-year anniversary of the Church's organization. During
that year PEF officers forgave debts of at least $337,000 for bor-
rowers considered worthy of help and too poor to pay. As part of
the backlash against the Church for polygamy and other perceived
sins, United States government officials disincorporated the
Perpetual Emigrating Company in the same legislation that disincorporated the Church. They also disenfranchised female members of the Church. During the late nineteenth century, opposition to the Church and its emigration program rose in crescendo
in the United States. Opposition also began in European nations
such as Norway, Denmark, and Sweden, from which converts
were immigrating to the United States. The United States also
tried to halt emigration to Utah, but it continued despite those
efforts. When the Perpetual Emigrating Fund was dissolved, it had
assets of $417,968.50, most in the form of promissory notes that
immediately lost most of their value when the government took
control of the fund.[21]

By the time PEF was dissolved, its purposes had largely been
fulfilled, and the people, including the poor, had come to the
western settlements, bringing their faith, skills, and a spirit of
community building. The Church had gained a firm toehold in
the Intermountain West.

Perhaps one example will serve to illustrate the far-reaching
effect a small loan made by PEF had on the activities and fortunes
of one family. We begin with a question and provide both the
answer and the experience.

What blind Scottish wood turner, of meager means, born in
Paisley, Scotland, in 1825, joined The Church of Jesus Christ of

Latter-day Saints on 5 February 1842, wanted to immigrate to join the body of the Saints in Utah, but could not raise the funds to make the long journey until 1862? The answer to the question is William Eccles.

The next question is: how did Eccles and the rest his family at last raise the money for the journey to Zion? And once they settled there, how did William's family fare in the valleys of Utah? The answers are of interest in considering the potential effect of the modern PEF.

William Eccles operated a wood lathe, making spools for spinners and weavers, first in Paisley, then in Glasgow. His widowed mother, Margaret Miller Eccles, found the means to join with the Saints in Nauvoo in 1843, one year after her baptism. Her letters home to Scotland exhorted her family to be faithful to the gospel. She died in 1845, long before her family could join her. William remained in Scotland. Eventually he and his wife, Sarah, moved both their business and their family to Glasgow where they were pillars in the Church while eking out a modest living for their family that included seven children. Their fifth child and second son was named David. At a very early age, David became a traveling merchant for his father's wood products. His business activities took him to other towns where he slept in doorways and hallways because he could not afford a bed.

Something of William's stalwart and optimistic character can be gleaned from his own statement about his near blindness. Said William: "If the Lord had so decreed that some men on earth must be blind, why then should it not be my lot to be one of them." William, along with the other members of the family, continued to work and serve and hope for a way to immigrate to Utah where he could join the body of the Church.

The constant frugal efforts of the Eccles family to save enough money to immigrate proved insufficient to finance the journey. This is not surprising. How could a nearly blind man with seven children, operating in a bleak economy, following the onset of the Industrial Revolution, raise enough money to pay for the long and arduous trip? To the Eccles family, America represented the land of opportunity and the home of faithful Latter-day Saints. Hadn't Brigham Young insisted that the faithful come to Zion!

After years of struggle and saving, the Eccles family was still far short of what it needed to immigrate. Then came the miracle. In April 1863, PEF advanced the sum of seventy-five pounds to William's son David. With what little the family had saved, this was barely enough to allow David and William to take the entire Eccles clan to Utah. They wasted no time in taking advantage of their good fortune. A mere two days after receiving the loan they departed from Glasgow with all their belongings, bound for Liverpool where the ship *Cynosure* awaited them and their fellow Mormon travelers. This began an incredible journey of more than four weeks across the Atlantic for the Eccleses and James Moyes, eldest son of William's sister. Arriving at Castle Gardens, New York, they embarked in railway cattle cars as far as existing rail could carry them. Horton David Haight (Elder David B. Haight's grandfather), a teamster by assignment of Brigham Young, captained the company of Saints across the plains. It must have been a long walk for blind William and 14-year-old David, but the family arrived safely in the Salt Lake Valley on 5 October 1863, four months after leaving Scotland.

Shortly after their arrival the family moved to Ogden. David, who had cut his teeth on commerce in Scotland, was destined to become a multi-millionaire as his abilities combined with business opportunities afforded in Utah and Oregon. After his mission back in Scotland, David and his business associates founded companies in such diverse industries as lumber, railroads, sugar beets, construction, banking, insurance, land and livestock, and mining. When he died on 10 December 1912, without a will, David's estate was estimated at 10 million dollars and more. After his death, a five-minute silent tribute was paid to Utah's wealthiest citizen by sugar beet factories, banks, streetcars, automobiles, and individuals.

What about the seventy-five pound loan? Was it repaid? The ledgers of the Church show that the family paid its loan in full by 1866. Without that loan the family could not have come to America and Utah, at least not when they did. Members of the Eccles family have made many contributions, both nationally and in Utah. One can hardly visit any campus, enter any civic building, or travel around the state of Utah without hearing about, observing, and enjoying the community contributions of the Eccles family. And it all started with a blind wood turner from Scotland. When one considers the far-reaching contributions of the old Perpetual Emigrating fund established by Brigham Young and his associates in 1849, one must marvel at their insight. The example of the Eccles family is just one of tens of thousands who came with the help of that fund.

1903

Next in the course of helping Church members rise above their circumstances was a somewhat forgotten educational initiative.

On 17 May 1903, the Church Board of Education established a fund for a very specific purpose, closely related to the modern PEF and a hint of what was to come in our day. Schoolteachers employed by the Church agreed to contribute one half of one percent of their salaries to a new loan fund. The board agreed to match the amount contributed by the teachers.

The purpose of the Education Fund was to promote advanced education among young Latter-day Saints. The Church was then located almost entirely in the Intermountain region. Those singled out for assistance were Church schoolteachers. The fund would help only those who lacked sufficient money to pursue their studies. The aid extended was in the form of loans, drawing a low rate of interest, to be repaid as soon as the borrower was able to do so. The officers of the fund kept careful accounts of the loans and subsequent repayments. These records reveal that many who availed themselves of this generous lending program provided valuable service in later years.

Roger Christensen, current secretary to the Church Board of Education at this writing, has possession of an accounting book that tracked these loans and repayments from 1903 until the early 1930s. He showed me the book, and it was fascinating to study the history of a program that anticipated what the Church is doing now. Because of its relevance, I showed the book to President Hinckley. He knew many of the recipients personally and immediately recognized the difference those small loans had made in the lives of the recipients. During his address at the general priesthood meeting held on 6 October 2001, President Hinckley said:

"Elder Carmack recently came across an old account book. He brought it to me. We discovered that way back in 1903, a small fund was established to help aspiring schoolteachers qualify for greater opportunities through small loans to assist them while going to school.

"It was continued for 30 years until it was finally dropped during the depression.

"I was amazed at the names contained in that old ledger book. Two became university presidents. Others became well known and highly qualified educators. The ledger shows repayments of $10.00, of $25.00, of $3.10 interest, and such things. One of the beneficiaries of that program became a bishop, then a stake president, then an Apostle, and eventually a counselor in the First Presidency.

"Brethren, we need to care for one another more diligently. We need to make a little more effort to assist those who are down at the bottom of the ladder. We need to give encouragement and a lifting hand to men and women of faith and integrity and ability, who can climb that ladder with a little help.

"That principle applies not only with reference to our present undertaking in this fund, but in a more general way. Let us open our hearts, let us reach down and lift up, let us open our purses, let us show a greater love for our fellowmen."[22]

Since the abandonment of the 1903 Education Fund, the Church has instituted other similar programs, but on a modest scale. These helped many of our young people gain an education but were not as ambitious as the comprehensive program that is today's PEF.

1936

The next major initiative designed to assist impoverished members of the Church was an ongoing program of assistance that has received well-deserved worldwide praise over the years. In his excellent book about the history of the Church Welfare Program, Elder Glen L. Rudd stated: "In April of 1936, the First Presidency of The Church of Jesus Christ of Latter-day Saints announced the inauguration of a welfare plan to care for the poor and needy of the Church."[23] This plan is generally well known in and out of the Church, but because it is such a major initiative in the work of helping disadvantaged members of the Church lift themselves, we touch lightly on it here.

As Elder Rudd explains, welfare work and programs did not begin in 1936, or even in 1830 when the Church was organized: "[Welfare work] is an inherent part of the gospel of Jesus Christ and has existed in one form or another whenever the gospel has been on the earth. The Lord has always required his Saints to establish some type of benevolent system to take care of the poor and those who are otherwise unable to care for themselves."[24]

In a special welfare meeting held on 3 August 1951, President J. Reuben Clark Jr. corroborated that fact: "[T]he Welfare Plan came through revelations that began in Adam's time and that have continued on until the present, and that the revelation which came to President Grant, in setting up the Welfare Plan, was merely to set up an organization which should be able to bring together, the United Order having passed away, the resources of the people to care for those who are in need."

President Clark added: "The Welfare Plan is based upon revelation, that the setting up of the machinery is the result of a revelation by the Holy Ghost to President Grant, that it has been carried on since that time by equivalent revelations which have come to the brethren who have had it in charge."[25]

What were the concerns that brought about the revelations establishing the welfare program, as we know it today? The 1930s saw a worldwide economic depression descend on the nations of the earth. This depression impacted the United States heavily. Unemployment reached staggering percentages, people were hungry, and despair was everywhere. Like other Americans, Latter-day Saints turned for help wherever they could get it, and at the height of the depression an estimated 80,000 members of the Church were on public relief. Out of work and out of hope, and dependent on small government doles, these people could see no apparent way out of their dependency on the government.

The First Presidency was, of course, greatly concerned for the Church and its members as well as for the people of the world. Leaders gave much time to prayer, fasting, and investigation on behalf of the Saints, and in the general conference held in April 1936, the First Presidency announced a program called the Church Security Plan. Prior to that time efforts to meet the crisis and help the poor were well underway in many stakes, but this was a plan that the Church would direct centrally from its headquarters in Salt Lake City. Powerful in its conception and vast in its scope, this inspired program and its underlying principles were described by the First Presidency in this well-known statement:

"Our primary purpose was to set up, in so far as it might be possible, a system under which the curse of idleness would be done away with, the evils of a dole abolished, and independence, industry, thrift and self respect be once more established amongst our people. The aim of the Church is to help the people to help themselves. Work is to be reenthroned as the ruling principle of the lives of our Church membership."[26]

Harold B. Lee was serving at the time as president of the Pioneer Stake in Salt Lake City. That stake had been especially impacted by economic hardship, and President Lee had been proactive in combating the effects of unemployment and despair among among its members. Recognizing his inspired leadership in this area, the First Presidency called President Lee to be the first managing director of the bold new initiative. President Heber J. Grant explained: "There was nothing more important for the Church to do than to take care of its needy people and that so far as he was concerned, everything else must be sacrificed [so that] proper relief [could be] extended to our people."[27] He explained that if necessary they would even close down the temples to take care of the Saints.[28]

Though extending help to the poor was not new, as we have seen, the scope, reach, and Church-wide emphasis on organizing to address the grave concerns of the times *were* new. True, the principles of brotherhood, sharing with those in need, working for what one received, and even the establishment of storehouses that bishops could use were already part of Church doctrine and practices, but now the Church would dedicate substantial resources to combating the devastating effects of poverty. In meeting these temporal needs, leaders would be governed by spiritual principles. President David O. McKay, who as a counselor in the First Presidency had much to do with implementing this program, explained: "It is something to supply clothing to the scantily clad, to furnish ample food to those whose table is thinly spread, to give activity to those who are fighting desperately the despair that comes from enforced idleness, but after all is said and done, the greatest blessings that will accrue from the Church Security Plan are spiritual."[29]

Speaking to stake presidents assembled at a special meeting on 2 October 1936, President J. Reuben Clark Jr. of the First Presidency made this classic statement: "The real long term objective of the Welfare Plan is the building of character in the members of the Church, givers and receivers, rescuing all that is finest down deep inside of them, and bringing to flower and fruitage the latent richness of the spirit, which after all is the mission and purpose and reason for being of this Church."[30]

Over and over, the leaders of the Church have affirmed that the Church Welfare Plan was the product of revelation. Though the program was specifically aimed at ameliorating difficult economic conditions faced by the Saints and others due to the worldwide depression, the principles upon which it is built are eternal and unchanging. So, while implementation has relieved the physical suffering of countless recipients, what is most impressive is the growth of faith and character that participants have experienced—both givers and recievers.

President Heber J. Grant, comes to mind first as the moving figure in establishing the program. The revelation came to him. In the early 1930s, responding to the assignment given to him by President Grant, President David O. McKay led out in implementing the welfare system. Then President J. Reuben Clark Jr. received the assignment when President Grant shifted responsibilities between his counselors. Elder Melvin J. Ballard was the first chairman of the General Welfare Committee. He literally wore himself out in promoting and establishing the program. As we have mentioned, the First Presidency called President Harold B.

Lee as the first managing director of the program. His work was well known, and his reputation in the field of welfare reached legendary proportions. Since then, countless leaders, both men of the priesthood and women of the Relief Society, have brought about miracles in administering a program for economic relief that remains today the envy of the world.

The foregoing vividly points out that the work of helping the poor is one eternal round. It has no beginning or end, but new applications come when we focus our attention and seek inspiration in order to meet great concerns. As the Perpetual Emigrating Fund and Company met the needs and concerns of bringing the poor to Zion, so in our day, President Gordon B. Hinckley and his associates have established the Perpetual Education Fund to help young people, especially returned missionaries, held down in grinding poverty, to rise out of difficult circumstances into the light of hope and opportunity.

The principles are the same, but regularly as circumstances dictate there is a need to apply them in important new ways. In the case of the Welfare Plan, what was needed was a centrally directed Church-wide program to harness the energies and resources of the Saints and put everyone to work. As a result of that great program, our vocabulary now includes such terms as *welfare canneries, Deseret Industries, Church farms, regional welfare centers, bishops' storehouses,* and *welfare regions.* In this program, as in all others, we find the opportunity for those possessing more than they need to voluntarily contribute to the relief of the poor. An integral part of the program is the privilege granted to all members to make fast-offering donations. The Church Welfare Program continues, ever expanding, as the Church grows and needs arise.

1946

In 1939, conflict commenced in Europe, eventually spreading and becoming World War II. The massive destruction of buildings, homes, entire cities, as well as the depletion of resources, left Europe in desperate straits. The Saints in Europe did not escape the ravages of the war. Many had lost their homes, been driven out of their communities, suffered the loss of loved ones, and scarcely had clothing to wear or food to put on their tables. Many faced literal starvation. The First Presidency knew that something needed to be done, and quickly. Ordinary measures were not enough. In addition to the suffering of the Saints, the Church organizational structure in the missions, districts, and branches was crippled. Contact with Church leadership had been lost during the war years. The First Presidency chose Elder Ezra Taft Benson of the Quorum of the Twelve to lead an unprecedented relief program in Europe and to preside over the European Mission. They asked him to leave his family during the year 1946 and rescue the Saints, reestablish the Church organization in Europe, and reopen the missions that had operated on a minimal basis during the war. That this work was part of the eternal round of the gospel is abundantly clear from this summary taken from the December 1945 issue of the *Improvement Era.*

"Little did the Prophet Joseph Smith realize when the Lord revealed to him the storehouse program for taking care of those in need that a hundred and fourteen years later it would mean the temporal salvation for his people in Europe. And little, too, did the members of the Church realize when the First Presidency announced in 1936 the organization of the welfare program to assist the bishops and the branch presidents in the discharge of their duties 'in searching after the poor to administer to their wants' that their work on welfare projects, in the production and storage of the necessities of life, would, in less than a decade, help to bring relief to a war-torn world."[31]

The First Presidency set apart Elder Benson for his new calling on Monday, 28 January 1946. He left home and family the next night. President George Albert Smith came to the Benson home to bid him farewell. Elder Harold B. Lee drove him to the airport where Elders Spencer W. Kimball, Mark E. Peterson, and Matthew Cowley, along with many others, said good-bye. Grounded by snow in Nebraska, forced to take a train to Chicago, and finding his flight to Europe postponed, he finally left the United States from New York City in a four-motored Clipper aircraft on 3 February 1946, landing in England. In London, mission president Hugh B. Brown met Elder Benson. Thus began a new chapter of assisting the Saints in their hour of need.

During 1946, Elder Benson traveled to virtually every corner of the war-ravaged countries of Europe from north to south and from east to west. He found the people in great need, but courageously coping with their circumstances. During the war the branches had carried on the work of the Lord as best they could, but the Church needed to be put in order. Elder Benson organized missions, installed new mission presidents, arranged for permission to bring missionaries back into the war-torn nations, and met with religious affairs departments and ambassadors. Obtaining visas was a constant problem and required much effort. Miracles abounded as the way opened when it seemed impossible.

He and those assisting him braved snowfall, fuel shortages, red tape, roadblocks, constant delays, misunderstandings, ravaged cities and highways, and tremendous shortages of food, especially fats, grains, and sugar, to rescue the Saints throughout Europe. Germany was especially hard hit, but shortages and starvation were present in nearly every country. Refugees from Eastern Europe flooded the western countries and added to the needs.

Trainloads and truckloads of food came from Church headquarters in Salt Lake City. It must have been gratifying when the food and supplies arrived at key points. But still, Elder Benson and his crew had to tackle and solve the problem of equitable distribution. The International Red Cross and the United States military were great partners in helping get commodities to those who so desperately needed them.

Elder Benson brought to the Saints not only much needed food and clothing, but also encouragement, hope, and faith. Wherever he went, he gathered the Saints into groups and testified to them that God was yet mindful of them and would bless them for their faithfulness. The Saints were overjoyed to see a General Authority, and tears of gratitude flowed. He fell in love with those Saints and they with him, for the relief he brought—both temporal and spiritual.

He visited the crematories and the concentration camps and saw firsthand the abomination of desolation brought about by the horrible conflict. He also found that during and after the war many of the Saints had experienced persecution for their religious beliefs. Rape, murder, plunder of homes, and confiscation of clothing, bedding, and animals were a reality to many of them. Sometimes they had to bury their belongings to save them. Many had to sell all they owned, just to sustain life. They also had to deal with the black market, in which cigarettes were the medium of exchange.

Homeless and displaced persons were on the move all over Europe, many of them relying on horses and wagons to move about. The slaughter of people in places like Poland, where millions of Jews had simply vanished, left those dealing with the aftermath horror-stricken. Filth and destruction were everywhere. Having seen their suffering and comprehending the unbelievable loss of life among them, Elder Benson developed a special love for the Jewish people.

The year of 1946 was critical in the temporal salvation of the European Saints, but the relief effort was only a continuation of efforts that had saved and helped the Lord's poor in the past. We think back to the flight from Missouri directed by the Twelve, the forced exodus from Nauvoo, and the migration across the plains—all accomplished with the needs of the poor uppermost in the minds of the leaders. Then came the Perpetual Emigrating Company and Fund, which brought tens of thousands of the poor from Europe to the valleys of Utah. That was followed by the welfare program, which grew out of the hard times spawned by the Great Depression. And when World War II devastated Europe, Elder Ezra Taft Benson accepted the duty laid upon him by the Brethren to mount yet another rescue mission.

In mid-November of 1946, Elder Alma Sonne, Assistant to the Twelve, arrived in Europe to relieve Elder Benson, who stayed until he had introduced Elder Sonne all over Europe and brought him fully up to date on the status of the work. Finally, Elder Benson arrived home on Friday, 13 December 1946, his tremendous mission accomplished and eternal bonds of love and brotherhood between him and the European Saints firmly established.

Now, as a related and logical next step, we are witnessing the rescue of returned missionaries and other Church members from poverty, through the Perpetual Education Fund and Department. The prophet has again remembered the poor in circumstances requiring a bold new initiative and organization. The Saints have always been ready to share what they have to rescue the poor and needy. Education is now the key. Truly the course of the Lord is one eternal round, and the round that is most needed today is to rescue those young adults who need education and training to rise out of their impoverished circumstances.

No one has better articulated the duty we have to care for the poor than Jacob in the Book of Mormon. Among the sins he condemned in his people was the pride that grew out of their love of riches and costly apparel and their indifference to the suffering of the needy. His counsel was: "Think of your brethren like unto yourselves, and be familiar with all and free with your substance, that they may be rich like unto you. But before ye seek for riches, seek ye for the kingdom of God. And after ye have obtained a hope in Christ ye shall obtain riches, if ye seek them; and ye will seek them for the intent to do good—to clothe the naked, and to feed the hungry, and to liberate the captive, and administer relief to the sick and the afflicted" (Jacob 2:17–19).

This is the same standard by which the modern Church and today's members will be judged. The eagerness and generosity with which Church members have greeted the Perpetual Education Fund is indeed good news and is an evidence that the Latter-day

Saints are not guilty of the selfishness that prevented Jacob's people from heeding the cries of the poor.

As we can clearly see, from the days of Joseph Smith to the days of Gordon B. Hinckley, the Lord has been unfailing in providing for the poor—revealing tailor-made initiatives to answer their concerns and meet their needs. In our day the need is education, and our loving Father has provided a way for that need to be met. Circumstances change, but the course of God truly is one eternal round.

NOTES

1. Joseph Smith, *History of The Church of Jesus Christ of Latter-day Saints,* ed. B. H. Roberts, 2d ed. rev., 7 vols. (Salt Lake City: The Church of Jesus Christ of Latter-day Saints, 1932–51), 3:250.

2. Ibid., 7:465.

3. Ibid., 7:464–65.

4. *Deseret News,* September 21, 1850. See also Journal History of The Church of Jesus Christ of Latter-day Saints, September 15, 1850, LDS Church Archives, Salt Lake City, Utah.

5. Perpetual Emigrating Fund Company Minutes, February 5, 1981, LDS Church Archives.

6. First Presidency (Brigham Young, Heber C. Kimball, Willard Richards) to Orson Hyde, October 16, 1849, in *Messages of the First Presidency of The Church of Jesus Christ of Latter-day Saints,* ed. James R. Clark, 6 vols. (Salt Lake City: Bookcraft, Inc., 1965–75), 2:39.

7. Seventh General Epistle, September 22, 1851, in *Messages,* 2:87–88.

8. Sixth General Epistle, September 22, 1851, in *Messages,* 2:87–88.

9. From Leonard J. Arrington, *Great Basin Kingdom: An Economic History of Latter-day Saints, 1830–1900* (Cambridge, Mass.: Harvard University Press, 1958), 99.

10. William Mulder, *Homeward to Zion: The Mormon Migration from Scandinavia* (Minneapolis, Minn.: University of Minnesota Press, 2000), 141–42.

11. James Linforth, ed., *Route from Liverpool to Great Salt Lake Valley, Illustrated with Steel Engravings and Wood Cuts from Sketches Made by Frederick Percy* (Liverpool: F. D. Richards, 1855), 19.

12. Charles Dickens, *The Uncommercial Traveller,* in *Leisure Hour Library* 57 (May 23, 1896): 82–83.

13. Journal History, April 8, 1849.

14. Linforth, ed., *Route from Liverpool,* 16–17.

15. *Journal of Discourses,* 26 vols. (Liverpool: Latter-day Saints' Book Depot, 1854–86), 3:4.

16. See Mulder, *Homeward to Zion.*

17. Brigham Young to George Q. Cannon, October 11, 1862, in Young Letterbooks, LDS Church Archives.

18. *Journal of Discourses,* 3:4.

19. Quoted in Mulder, *Homeward to Zion,* 154.

20. Christian A. Madsen to John Van Cott, July 14, 1861, in Scandinavian Mission General History, unpublished manuscript, LDS Church Archives.

21. See Richard L. Jensen, "Names of Persons and Sureties Indebted to the Perpetual Emigrating Fund Company 1850–1877," *Mormon Historical Studies* 1, no. 2 (Fall 2000): 141–241.

22. Conference Report, October 2001, 69.

23. Glen L. Rudd, *Pure Religion: The Story of Church Welfare Since 1930* (Salt Lake City: Deseret Book, 1995), 1.

24. Ibid.

25. "Testimony of Divine Origin of Welfare Plan," *Church News,* August 8, 1951, 13, 15.

26. Conference Report, October 1936, 3.

27. Rudd, *Pure Religion,* 40.

28. Ibid., 34.

29. Conference Report, October 1936, 103.

30. Quoted in Rudd, *Pure Religion,* 44.

31. "The Church Welfare Program Helps European Saints," *Improvement Era* 48 (December 1945): 747.

Andres and Adriana Maria, Colombia

Andres works a full week, earning about $125 per month, and attends school fulltime as well. Adriana does what she can to help while awaiting their first baby. Full of faith and serving in responsible Church callings, they look forward to a ten-fold increase in income when Andres graduates next year in telecommunications. Their first financial goal? "We hope to refurbish an old van on our street and take the whole neighborhood to Church!"

CHAPTER THREE

"WHAT ARE YOUR PLANS?"

*In the service of the Lord, it is not where
you serve but how. In the Church of Jesus Christ
of Latter-day Saints, one takes the place to
which one is duly called, which place
one neither seeks nor declines.*

PRESIDENT J. REUBEN CLARK JR., GENERAL CONFERENCE, 9 APRIL 1951

CHURCH MEMBERS THROUGHOUT the world had heard the announcement and caught the vision concerning PEF. Calls and letters immediately started pouring into Church headquarters from young adults wanting to apply for loans and become PEF recipients. There was no time to lose. Church members also had resonated to President Hinckley's identification of the problem and his vision for its inspired solution. They wanted and expected it to be up and running, and now.

Let us step back about two months. The story begins in Frankfurt, Germany, where I was serving in the area presidency for the Europe Central Area of the Church. My scheduled date for completion of active service in the Seventy was to be October conference of that year, 2001. I expected to complete my assignment and be granted emeritus status during general conference.

On 11 February 2001, everything in my life turned upside

down. My wife and I were home in our cozy Frankfurt duplex on Tannenweg in the early evening when a call came from President Gordon B. Hinckley. Such a call from the prophet is not only rare, but it also serves to capture your full attention. After asking me what I was planning to do when I became emeritus, the President said he had a matter to discuss with me. He began by describing a condition in the world and in the Church that concerned the Brethren. The Church missionary program, as we have already seen, now included service by young men and women whose homes were in less-advantaged, poor countries of the world. He explained that the Church called these young men and women to serve as missionaries for a period of time, usually a year and a half for women and two years for men, and when they completed that service they routinely returned to their homes and countries to face serious poverty and lack of opportunity for meaningful employment. Some of these missionaries, he explained, thus left a period of giving vital and meaningful service, performed with all of their hearts, only to face hopelessness, poverty, and lack of means to gain education to relieve their poverty. Education, knowledge, and training in some skill or trade could in many or most cases open employment opportunities for them and lead them out of poverty, but most could not afford the cost of such education.

Having served in many less-advantaged countries, including such diverse nations as India, Mongolia, Pakistan, Haiti, Bangladesh, and many others, I knew firsthand the conditions President Hinckley described and agreed completely with his concern for our young people from those areas. He then described a new initiative that would address, at least in part, the problem. He intended to introduce it at general conference in a month and a half.

Before sharing the details of the new initiative, he described a similar need the Church had faced in the nineteenth century. Missionaries, especially in Great Britain and Scandinavia, were bringing large numbers of converts into the Church by the 1850s and '60s. These new converts, many of whom were poor, desperately wanted to join the body of the Church that was just establishing itself in the mountains and valleys of America's West, but they lacked the means to finance the journey to America and across the United States by wagon train or handcart to the Utah Territory. The Church needed these faithful members to help establish new communities and provide skilled labor, but how could they finance the journey?

President Hinckley then described the nineteenth century solution to the problem the Church then faced. Brigham Young and his associates decided to create a new fund called the Perpetual Emigrating Fund (PEF) and a new company called the Perpetual Emigrating Company to administer the fund and program of emigration. This new organization would provide loans that would enable converts to leave Europe and come to Utah. Over a period of nearly twenty years, some 30,000 Church members came to Salt Lake City and surrounding valleys with the help of loans from the old PEF. Despite being poor themselves, members who were already settled contributed money and other goods to create the fund and keep it alive. Brigham Young replenished the fund when necessary by transferring tithing resources to PEF and borrowing money from banks to keep the emigrants coming.

Then, changing to the present need, President Hinckley

described the creation of a new and modern initiative that would start with the creation of a fund to be called the Perpetual Education Fund, borrowing its name and abbreviation from the former PEF. This fund would provide loans to less-advantaged young adults, particularly returned missionaries, to finance training and education. The education would be largely vocational and technical in nature, leading to employment that would substitute hope and opportunity for hopelessness and poverty.

President Hinckley then described the organization: a board of directors, chaired by the Church President, would head the modern PEF. The President's counselors and others would serve on the board. The board would oversee this new initiative. I had no idea yet why President Hinckley was telling me about this great new initiative, but I knew this wasn't a social call.

I then discovered the reason for his call. To create and handle the business of this initiative, a new department was to be organized—one that would administer the fund and process the loans and repayments. In his good-natured style, President Hinckley explained that they had in mind an emeritus General Authority to manage the new department. That person, he said, was in Germany but was to attend 171st annual general conference in April, then stay home to take up his new labors. Then he issued a call for me to serve in this new responsibility. Surprised and shocked, I nevertheless found words to respond on behalf of Shirley and myself. We would, of course, accept that assignment and arrange our affairs to return to Salt Lake City in late March 2001, as directed.

Shirley and I slept little that night, thinking about the exciting new vision from our prophet. The task of helping create a practical reality out of the vision rested immediately and heavily on our shoulders, tempering our excitement. Our minds were awhirl with the difficult road that lay ahead.

Many duties awaited us during the months of April through the end of July, before our regularly scheduled departure from Germany. My secretary, Ann Steele, had just carefully planned a two-week trip to the Middle East where we would hold conferences. She had painstakingly obtained all the visas that are required for such a trip. We were also in the midst of launching construction of a new temple in the Netherlands. I had stake conferences and reorganizations on my mind and schedule. My associates in the work, Elders D. Lee Tobler and Ronald A. Rasband, would have to take over most of my assignments after we left. Fortunately, we also had other seventy, local men of proven ability, who could share the load. It would all work, but it would take some doing.

During the next couple of weeks, my mind and heart turned often to the new assignment. I was painfully aware that we could hurt rather than help these young people if we failed to build PEF on sound fundamentals of honor, self-reliance, commitment, integrity, and if we weren't able to find a way to help recipients of these loans plan and accomplish realistic and attainable goals.

General Authorities who are assigned overseas and who attend general conference have small temporary offices and secretarial help provided to carry on with their work in area presidencies around the world. The problems don't rest just because the leaders are away. My fellow area presidency members and I still had the duties associated with giving leadership in the vast Europe Central Area.

There were other demands. Most of the Saints would be surprised to observe the intense training of the General Authorities and staff that accompanies general conference and is an important part of it. Arriving in Salt Lake City, we were immediately caught up in attending these various leadership sessions. In addition, I was to be one of the speakers in the Sunday afternoon general session of conference, an assignment that weighed heavily on me. I hardly had time to breathe.

At one of the first of these training meetings, I chanced to see President James E. Faust of the First Presidency. He was one of the few who knew of my new calling and responsibility. With a twinkle in his eye, he said, "John, what did you ever do in the pre-existence to deserve such a calling?" It was his good-natured way of acknowleging the size of the task that lay before me. Then he added: "Sometimes an opportunity comes your way, perhaps once in a lifetime, to truly do something that will make a difference in people's lives. That has happened to you. If you seize the opportunity you can render a great service to thousands of people."

My appreciation for his expression was tempered by the added feeling of responsibility it conveyed. How in the world could I do what was asked of me? At the same time, having served extensively at both the local and general level of Church government, I knew that I would not be alone in this work and that the Lord did not intend for this bold initiative to fail. My greatest need would be to be humble, prayerful, diligent, and try to measure up.

When general conference concluded on Sunday afternoon and I had delivered my own talk, I felt a great sense of relief. I would nominally remain president of the Europe Central Area until 15 August and needed to keep in touch with the work there, but my capable counselors would shoulder most of that load. Except for weekend stake conference assignments in the United States and Canada, the last such assignments I would have before becoming an emeritus General Authority, I was free to put virtually my whole time, thought, prayer, and effort into making President Hinckley's vision a reality.

Being home brought us much joy, especially to Shirley. As we contended with jetlag and adjusted to the changes, we found time to see friends and enjoy visits with our family and neighbors. Assignments to host out-of-town guests, such as the Iceland Ambassador, continued. The General Authorities and their wives enjoyed a sacrament meeting together on 3 April. Soon-to-be-emeritus and retiring members of the Seventy administered and passed the sacrament to the congregation that was limited to General Authorities and their wives. I participated in that honor since it was to be my last such meeting. We learned during the conference that Elder Marlin K. Jensen would join Elders D. Lee Tobler and Ronald A. Rasband in the Europe Central Area Presidency on 15 August. Shirley and I hosted Sisters Amelia McConkie and Ethelynn Taylor at the Seventies Quorums social held on the 26th floor of the Church Office Building. We were doing many things for the last time; our lives were clearly changing.

KARLA, GUATEMALA

Inspired by a PEF fireside, Karla received guidance at the Institute of Religion and determined she could gain an education *without* a PEF loan. With help from the LDS Employment Resources Center, she found a great job with a pharmaceutical company and she is paying her own way through school. Her employer summarized his evaluation in simple terms: "Send me more Mormons!"

CHAPTER FOUR

LIFE AND THE SCRIPTURES POINT THE WAY

I give unto you a commandment, that you rely upon the things which are written.

DOCTRINE AND COVENANTS 18:3

SURELY THE ABILITY TO FEEL compassionate comes from above and from the example of those who rear us. The example of kind, compassionate parents is a rich source of such feelings, and the scriptures point the way as well. Personal circumstances are key, for certain periods of our lives provide greater opportunities for reaching out and lifting up struggling souls. The decade of the 1930s stands out as one such time.

I grew up in the 1930s in Winslow, Arizona. Almost everyone who lived in our ward and community would be considered poor by today's standards. Yet, we were fortunate to always enjoy enough food to eat. Our mother ran the household; she was a wonderful homemaker and a good cook. Our father owned and operated his own business, an auto mechanic shop. He was able and hardworking, but money was scarce. Even though we were all of modest or poor means in Winslow, there was still a division between those who had enough and those who struggled to find a way to survive. The poorest lived in certain sections of town.

My father taught me a great lesson when I was growing up there. Our next-door neighbor was Mrs. Daughwalter, a German immigrant with a heavy accent. As you might imagine, that accent was not a favored one in 1939 and 1940 with the Nazis terrorizing Europe and World War II on the horizon.

The neighborhood children, including me, made fun of her accent. She lived alone and was an easy target, and we loved to laugh at her peculiar speech and seized opportunities to taunt her. Hearing the harmful gossip the neighborhood children indulged in, my father took me aside for a talk. "Don't you know that Mrs. Daughwalter is getting older, that she is a fine person and an excellent neighbor? I want you to treat her with respect and help the other children in the neighborhood do the same."

During our family's last winter in Arizona and just before we moved to California in 1942, Mrs. Daughwalter became seriously ill. She was unable to even get out of bed to light a fire or cook meals. Father took over, appointing me—as the oldest of the boys—to assist. "John Kay, I want you to bring in wood and coal every morning and make Mrs. Daughwalter's fire."

The dividend from the care our family took of her was great. She was grateful to our mother, who prepared her meals, and credited our father with saving her life that winter. In broken English, she often expressed her gratitude and love to me, revealing a pure heart and good person. She became a close friend to the Carmack family, and after we moved to California, she continued to mail German candies and cookies to us until her death.

After we moved from Arizona to California, our father

engaged in pursuits connected with the war effort. And because of hard work, ability, and an improving economy, we moved gradually from subsistence to abundance. Our parents never forgot, however, to look after the needs of the less fortunate. To the end of her life, our mother would take lunch to our father at work and stay and take care of the books. On the way to his machine shop, she would frequently stop to provide hope, food, and friendship to people in need. And our father always sought out those who needed friends and help as well. Such examples of simple but meaningful service are extremely powerful in shaping the character and attitudes of impressionable children.

Beyond the teachings we receive at home by example, the feelings of caring, sharing, and looking after the needs of others surely come from a divine source. It was a key tenet in Christ's teachings to care for the needy, the downtrodden, and the hopeless: "For I was an hungered, and ye gave me meat: I was thirsty, and ye gave me drink: I was a stranger, and ye took me in: Naked, and ye clothed me: I was sick, and ye visited me: I was in prison, and ye came unto me. Then shall the righteous answer him, saying, Lord, when saw we thee an hungred, and fed thee? or thirsty, and gave thee drink? When saw we thee a stranger, and took thee in? or naked, and clothed thee? Or when saw we thee sick, or in prison, and came unto thee? And the King shall answer and say unto them, Verily I say unto you, Inasmuch as ye have done it unto one of the least of these my brethren, ye have done it unto me" (Matthew 25:35–40).

The great outpouring of love and a genuine desire to share that people have shown in the past years have deeply touched those of us who are directly involved in establishing PEF.

Donations to the fund have come not only from wealthy people and from organizations with an abundance of assets, but from children, people of modest means, and friends of the Church.

In this outpouring of generosity and concern, the Spirit of Christ, the Light of the World, may be seen. Many who routinely only prayed for "the poor and the needy among us," have been prompted to respond to the prophet's invitation to contribute to PEF. Something fine inside of us, something we undoubtedly brought from our premortal home, where we lived in the presence of our Heavenly Father, teaches, reminds, and urges us to watch out for the poor among us.

The importance of ministering to the needy is clearly taught in the scriptures. In fact, the prophets have sternly admonished us to take care of the poor or face the consequences of a hellish afterlife. These are harsh reminders of our duty, and we might well ask ourselves why is failure to care for the poor so terrible? Isn't it a sin of omission rather than an outright transgression of the law of God?

In latter-day scriptures, we find a compelling explanation of why the Lord requires us to care for the poor. Section 104 of the Doctrine and Covenants tells us that as the Creator of this rich and beautiful earth, the Lord is the rightful owner of all of its treasures and resources. Though we are permitted to be stewards of its bounties, everything on and in the earth belongs to Him. In his mercy and wisdom, He has provided amply for our needs, "For the earth is full, and there is enough and to spare" (D&C 104:17), and those who have garnered a portion of its wealth through industry or good fortune are expected by the Lord to give of their abundance to help the less fortunate. "Therefore, if any man shall take of the abundance which I have made, and impart not his portion, according to the law of my gospel, unto the poor and the needy, he shall, with the wicked, lift up his eyes in hell, being in torment" (D&C 104:18).

This has been a law to God's people from the earliest times of man's sojourn on earth. Some have lived this law more perfectly than others. Among the inhabitants of the ancient city of Enoch, a city taken from the earth because of its righteousness and perfection, there were no poor (see Moses 7:18). Following my appointment, I read these and hundreds of other verses with new interest and renewed insight. What a breathtaking vision our prophet has opened to us! And the responsibility that descends on us—to be pioneers in establishing a fund aimed at providing assistance to less-advantaged young Church members around the globe—is so vast in scope and potential for good that I was scarcely able to quit thinking about it day or night.

I have often reflected on the story Jesus told of the rich young man who came by night, seeking advice regarding his eternal welfare. He must have learned something of the plan of salvation through prior contact with either Jesus or one of his disciples. Now, granted an audience with the Master, he asked Jesus the question that worried him. What an opportunity it would be for any one of us to be able to ask Jesus a question face to face! The rich young man had that inestimable privilege. We are indebted to him for his question, because he asked not just for himself, but also for all of us, "Dear Savior, what must I do to inherit eternal life?" (see Matthew 19:16–22). The question was to the point and relevant to all of us.

The Savior answered by saying that he must keep the commandments of God. "Which ones?" asked the young man. The

Savior patiently enumerated the key commandments: commit no murder, don't engage in adultery, and don't steal or bear false witness. Those were commandments to not do forbidden acts. Then Christ gave him two affirmative commandments to keep: honor your father and your mother, and love your neighbor as yourself.

The young man's answer was that he had kept all of these commandments from his youth to the present. He was apparently a fine person, one possessing admirable traits and qualities. But had he left the interview at that, we would not have learned the crucially important principles that Jesus added. The young man asked Him: "What lack I yet?"

Jesus responded: "If thou wilt be perfect, go and sell that thou hast, and give to the poor, and thou shalt have treasure in heaven: and come and follow me" (Matthew 19:21). This is hard doctrine, for it is difficult for anyone to give away all of one's worldly goods. How many of us could pass that test if asked?

This enlightening tale ends with the young man departing in a state of sorrow because he had great possessions that apparently meant so much to him that it would be wrenching for him to part with them. Surely, even without the suggested sacrifice, he would be blessed for all he had done from his youth up. We never learn what happened to the rich young man. It is possible that pride took him away from the discipleship that he had begun to enjoy. I prefer to think and hope that the Savior's answer worked on him to the point that he overcame his love of wealth and became a faithful follower of Jesus and the gospel.

From what we have seen in establishing PEF, many have the spirit and attitude that would enable them to pass Jesus' test. That is encouraging when we think of the incredible wealth existing in the more advanced countries of the world. People desiring to help have come to us anonymously, bringing that kind of spirit with them. We need to cultivate a broken heart and a contrite spirit, and a willingness to give our all if asked. This includes our own lives. We are told in this dispensation: "Wherefore, fear not even unto death; for in this world your joy is not full, but in me your joy is full. Therefore, care not for the body, neither the life of the body; but care for the soul, and the life of the soul" (D&C 101:36–37).

In one area in which I served as area president, a good friend who had been very successful in business invited me to his office for a beautifully set lunch—just for the two of us. We talked of the work of the Church, of the teachings of President Hinckley, and of this friend's success in business. He showed me his offices and described his holdings. Then he said: "You are my priesthood leader. If you ever need all or part of my worldwide assets for the work of the Lord, you let me know and they will be available—all of them." There is something fine in the Latter-day Saints, and now with PEF established we are finding a noble and great way to minister to the poor. Surely the motivation to do so comes from above.

One story Jesus told that haunts and teaches us is that of Lazarus and the rich man:

"There was a certain rich man, which was clothed in purple and fine linen, and fared sumptuously every day:

"And there was a certain beggar named Lazarus, which was laid at his gate, full of sores,

"And desiring to be fed with the crumbs which fell from the rich man's table: moreover the dogs came and licked his sores.

"And it came to pass, that the beggar died, and was carried by the angels into Abraham's bosom: the rich man also died, and was buried;

"And in hell he lift up his eyes, being in torment, and seeth Abraham afar off, and Lazarus in his bosom.

"And he cried and said, Father Abraham, have mercy on me, and send Lazarus, that he may dip the tip of his finger in water, and cool my tongue; for I am tormented in this flame.

"But Abraham said, Son, remember that thou in thy lifetime receivedst thy good things, and likewise Lazarus evil things: but now he is comforted, and thou art tormented.

"And beside all this, between us and you there is a great gulf fixed: so that they which would pass from hence to you cannot; neither can they pass to us, that would come from thence" (Luke 16:19–26).

The beautiful language of the King James Bible provides us with that classic story. Someone has said that the scriptures that he understands perfectly well are the ones that bother him the most. We don't need to dwell on this one too much; we understand it only too well. The sins of omission of the rich man are easy to spot, and these shortcomings had, at least in the story, a terrible and frightening impact on his life after death. Still, that story is so relevant to all of us that we need to stop and remember it from time to time. Many Latter-day Saints are in no danger of suffering the rich man's fate. Those of us involved in managing PEF have been humbled by the number of rank-and-file Church members who have voluntarily responded to President Hinckley's invitation to support this program of outreach to our young people in poverty.

Early on in establishing the PEF program and department,

my colleagues and I were excited to discover the applicability of a little-known parable found in the Doctrine and Covenants. The moving story is told in only one verse and describes a father who had twelve sons. These twelve sons were all obedient, serving their father in love and respect. The father, as is true with most of us who have children, respected and loved his twelve sons equally. The Savior asked us a question concerning the treatment that the father should afford his sons. If the man should say to one group of his sons, "I want you to have the finest clothing and education that money can buy" but say to another group of his sons, "You must wear only rags and don't ask for any help in preparing for employment and opportunities in life," could the father look in the mirror and say, "I am a just father?" (see D&C 38:26).

The answer to the question is obvious and teaches a powerful lesson. We all try to be fair, with whatever means are at our disposal, as we raise our children. If we imagine the father in the parable to be the Prophet and President of The Church of Jesus Christ of Latter-day Saints, we can begin to understand in some small way the passionate feelings President Hinckley has about the need for this new program. And I testify that members of the Church have caught the spirit of it. Many have been moved by the vision and want to help in such a cause.

Next let's remind ourselves of some teachings associated with the creation of the world, as revealed to us in the books of Moses and Abraham in the Pearl of Great Price. According to what is revealed there, Heavenly Father planned the creation carefully and implemented those plans through a council that carried out His instructions. The earth when it was formed contained an abundance of everything necessary to sustain life—an atmosphere, vegetation, animal life, rich soil, precious ores, and useful elements, especially water. Since He was its creator, the earth and all things therein belong to Him. As already noted, there is enough and to spare on the earth for all of us to live well, despite theories of some men to the contrary. God has given the inhabitants of the earth, His spiritually begotten children, the gift of agency, which gives us the right and obligation to choose wisely for the good of each other. He intends that his people share with each other, so that everyone will have the opportunity to live well. But some of us end up with more than others, and some have less than is essential to an abundant life. He expects us—out of love and concern for our neighbors—to share resources and help people. (This doctrine is taught in power and simplicity in section 104:14–17 of the Doctrine and Covenants.)

There are many references in the scriptures that teach us our responsibility as stewards of the wealth of this world. The Nephites frequently failed in this respect, their pride and love of things bringing them down. On some occasions in the history of God's dealings with his children, one wise and inspired man has preserved whole nations, as Joseph did in saving Egypt, his father's tribe, and all the surrounding nations through his judicious storage of surpluses in times of plenty and his careful distribution of stored food in times of scarcity.

The Lord instructed Moses that the Israelites were to take care of their poor. He outlined a simple program of forgiving debts on a regular and consistent basis and admonished them to leave a residue of their crops in the corners of their fields so that the poor could glean needed food for their sustenance following harvest. They were not to gather every grape, but remember both the poor and the stranger that needed food (see Leviticus 19:9–10). As an example of this charitable program, we read about Ruth, a Moabite, who was saved from hunger and poverty by gleaning the field of its wealthy owner, a near kinsman, who later married her. Thus Boaz showed the charity and benevolence expected of an Israelite, and Ruth was preserved to take her place in the royal genealogical line of Jesus as recorded in Matthew.

The principles that underlie the PEF are just and true and in keeping with the divine decree that we minister to the poor and needy. We have been thrilled to observe how many of the rank-and-file members of the Church immediately caught the vision of this work and voluntarily gave of their resources in answer to President Hinckley's plea to help a new generation of young adults rise out of poverty. Many of us have been successful in our temporal lives, and most of us rightfully feel that we are merely stewards of what the Lord has allowed us to have. We have received many letters from the Saints, expressing that understanding of their stewardship and seeking to help without undermining the self-reliance or destroying the self-esteem of those we help. We want to help and not hurt those needing a helping hand.

The Perpetual Education Fund is based on sound principles that are imbedded deep inside us. In that inspired initiative many of us have seen one way to fulfill our earnest desire to lift the hands that hang down and succor the poor. In participating in this great and noble enterprise, we are not only nurturing individuals but helping to expand the Lord's work as the restored gospel of Jesus Christ continues its phenomenal growth in the nations of the world.

DOUGLAS, EL SALVADOR

Douglas is studying refrigeration engineering, one of the jobs in great demand in Central America. Still in school, he already has several clients thanks to his excellent reputation. He will soon open his own shop.

CHAPTER FIVE

BUILDING A TEAM AND A
FIRM FOUNDATION

*Except the Lord build the house,
they labor in vain that build it.*

PSALM 127:1

THE FOLLOWING PAGES DESCRIBE the creation of the Perpetual Education Fund and a Church department to administer it. The story begins with the closing of the annual general conference in early April 2001. On Wednesday morning, 4 April, I felt alone with nothing but great expectations. Where was I to turn for help and what should my first step be? Knowing I needed to begin work immediately, I went to the Church Administration Building where the First Presidency has its offices. I called on Don Staheli, President Hinckley's personal secretary. He arranged for me to see President Hinckley. Within half an hour President Hinckley had directed Elder L. Tom Perry of the Twelve to find an office for me, dictated directions to several of the Brethren to assist in setting up this new department to be called the Perpetual Education Fund Department, and given me instructions on how to proceed. He told me that he would call the new board of directors together

75

soon and arrange a formal announcement of my appointment as managing director of the Perpetual Education Fund. Things were happening quickly. The vision was moving to a beginning.

Elder Perry placed me in room 950 in the Church Office Building, the former office of the Church Commissioner of Education. It was a large suite that I later divided into two offices for one of our PEF associates to share. I obtained the use of a computer and moved in on Monday, 9 April.

One of my first acts was to purchase a new set of scriptures. I wanted to read them with this new calling in mind, without distractions from other markings. Available to me in the adjoining CES offices were the supplies and materials used by CES leaders and secretaries. This office placement seemed appropriate and providential because of the close partnership that would be required between the PEF and CES in implementing the work of our department. The next day, 10 April, Garry Moore of CES showed me around the office and introduced me to the headquarters CES staff. That staff administers a global program of education that is perhaps the largest in the world. Garry gave me a primer on how they operate. Then Stanley A. Peterson, leader of Church religious education (seminaries, institutes of religion, and Church schools), spent an hour describing the way they were organized and how they carried out their work. I became reacquainted with a modest program of loans and grants being given to institute students. This program, called the International Education Fund (IEF), operated in less-advantaged countries. I had been aware of it while serving in Asia in the early 1990s. Started in 1973, the CES had made loans and grants to thousands of institute students, many of them returned missionaries. It was obvious to both of us that the old IEF program would have to be coordinated with the new PEF loan program. The IEF program, as it was then constituted, would have to be phased out, but there were many promises to keep and expectations to meet before that could happen.

PEF now had a home. I moved things around a bit in the office and gathered the materials needed to run a headquarters function. Stan Peterson offered to share the services of Janis Loveland, his fine secretary, until I could find one of my own. I was kept busy answering letters, performing temple marriages for close friends, and preparing a speech for the LDS Business College graduation. My first stake conference since reassignment was in Edmonton, Alberta, Canada. I set about getting my computer and software installed and went to work in the pleasing environment created by CES.

The Brethren sent over a proposed *Church News* article announcing my appointment. I read, edited, and approved it. Now news of my appointment would gradually spread around the Church. Weekly quorum meetings for the Seventy, something we miss when serving overseas, occupied some time each week. By the end of my first week I could sense some progress. We had set up an office and learned more about the responsibilities that lay ahead. I had met with members of the Twelve who would serve on the board of directors, visited with Elder Aldin Porter and Stan Peterson who were on the board, given an interview with a reporter from the *Church News,* and kept Janis Loveland, my temporary secretary, busy preparing letters and documents.

Because so many adjustments have to be made as you come and go, we found that returning home after some years absence is, in many ways, harder than leaving the country on assignment. At home we reacquainted ourselves with neighbors and ward members. The days in the office, busy with little details and preparation for establishing PEF, went by quickly. I knew that I needed some assistance and began to think about where I might look for volunteers.

Thus far I had found that as soon as I thought about a need or concern, the way was opened to meet the need or solve the concern. On the question of finding someone to help me, Elders M. Russell Ballard and Henry B. Eyring of the PEF board of directors called to invite me to Elder Ballard's office where I was introduced to Chad L. Evans. Chad's involvement with PEF and the events of his life leading up to his selection to be part of the team can best be told in his own words:

> Almost immediately following President Hinckley's announcement that the Church was creating a new department and fund, Elder Carmack called me to serve as director of operations for the Perpetual Education Fund. Not only has this been a marvelous service opportunity for my family and me, but has added evidence to my conviction that life is a gift with meaningful purpose. I feel that can be true for everyone. I wanted to share the feelings and experiences leading my wife, Karen, and me to this service. Some of the experiences are sacred, private, and confidential, but most can be shared.
>
> Karen and I have owned and operated businesses in a number of industries, including mining, electronics,

and services related to technology and the computer industry. Despite the satisfactions and successes derived from these endeavors, we began about 1980 to feel that just owning and operating businesses for profit did not completely fulfill our desire to help and serve people, particularly young people, in more direct and meaningful ways. Our thoughts had more and more turned toward those of meager means in the world, and we wanted to find some way to be involved in assisting them.

We began in a small way at first. We turned from industry toward investing time and money in community colleges and vocational schools that trained young and old alike in vocational and technical skills leading directly to better employment opportunities. The more involved with education we became, the more satisfaction we felt with our involvement. Thus we turned more and more of our effort in that direction, little realizing where this would lead us. Looking back we can see that those efforts were leading inexorably in the direction of what we are now engaged in doing with PEF. In the process of these activities, we gained in-depth knowledge about vocational and technical education, and added understanding about how to attract and help recruit students to these schools. Although the schools were organized for profit, they were wonderfully relevant to the needs of the students and the communities they served. We discovered that we could and did meet the needs of thousands of young people.

This feeling of satisfaction in helping young people and the knowledge and experience we acquired in the process led us to form a business whose purpose was primarily recruiting students for hundreds of colleges and training organizations. We learned how to help students dream, plan, obtain loans, and achieve their goals. We were finding purpose in our lives beyond simply reaching our own financial goals. And we were, in the process, learning much about career development and how to open avenues of opportunity for young people to achieve their dreams.

About that time, a good friend who managed employment services for the Church talked to us about initiatives the Church was pursuing to assist young people and others to find employment. In particular, we focused on what additional untapped avenues could provide new opportunities for our returned missionaries and others. In time this led us to simplify our business activities. Doing so enabled me to accept opportunities offered to spend most of my working hours helping in such things as welfare and humanitarian services, establishing employment resource centers, brainstorming new and additional opportunities for young people, and actually planning ways to achieve goals in these areas. The financial success we enjoy in our various businesses allowed me to donate virtually my full time to these efforts. Inner feelings and desire drove me to learn all I could about the goals of the Church and mechanisms that would allow the Church to achieve those goals. Serving in the Church environment required patience for one accustomed to being the decision maker, but I felt driven by a keen desire to persevere in that direction.

At the same time, my interest extended to learn all I could about world organizations dedicated to eradicating poverty and assisting the very poor to become self-reliant and successful business owners. I learned the principles behind successfully loaning small amounts of capital to people and helping them achieve independence by repaying that which they had borrowed. Thus I spent my days serving with and learning from those of little or no means. As I learned, I shared my ideas about these matters with my associates in the Church.

Even before President Hinckley announced and explained the Perpetual Education Fund in the general priesthood meeting, I had the distinct feeling that all my wife and I had been doing to help less-advantaged young people was leading to something we would and must become involved with in a major way. I saw, with what I can only describe as my spiritual eyes, major opportunities ahead to assist and serve in new initiatives that I felt were coming—something of immense value and importance in the lives of young people desperate for opportunities and in need of help.

Then came the great announcement about the Perpetual Education Fund on 31 March 2001. I was there, and I was moved beyond my power to explain or understand what was happening. I seemed to have an instant testimony and understanding of the principles President Hinckley declared that evening. Many of my own thoughts about how we could truly make a difference in the lives of young adults, particularly those in areas impacted by poverty, exactly coincided with President Hinckley's explanations on that memorable evening.

When the First Presidency announced that Elder Carmack would be the managing director of PEF, I somehow knew I would be involved, even though I didn't know Elder Carmack. Soon, however, Church leaders who knew both of us brought us together in a meeting where we could exchange ideas about how to bring President Hinckley's vision into a full and practical program. These announced initiatives would require planning, organization, and leadership. I very much desired to be involved.

Soon Elder Carmack obtained approval through regular channels to call me as his assistant. My immediate acceptance put me in another position to further fulfill the purposes for which my wife and I had been prepared. We who formed that initial team, organized to bring about the noble purposes of the Perpetual Education Fund, seem to have been brought together providentially. At least we felt that way. The task was huge, and we felt overwhelmed and humble; but we also felt immense gratitude for the tremendous responsibilities that devolved upon us. We have felt that very specific purposes have been at work in our lives, not just recently, but for many years, leading us to this point. All credit for anything we have achieved thus far must go to the Lord and His prophet.

Chad Evans was uniquely qualified by his experiences in life to be useful in his calling. Still in his forties, he was ready to share what he knew and his tremendous energy. He had no immediate need for income to support his family and had watched the emergence of the PEF with great interest. In addition, he had learned much about how the Church operated internally at headquarters and in the field. In doing all of that he had gained the confidence of many in Church headquarters. After interviewing Chad, I quietly arranged with all necessary parties to present his name to the board of directors as a volunteer director for PEF.

On 17 April, I received a letter signed by the First Presidency, confirming my call as managing director of the Perpetual Education Fund and Department. The letter included notice of the first meeting of the board, scheduled for 2:00 P.M. on Wednesday, 25 April 2001, in the First Presidency's council room. The letter stated: "We are confident that the work of the board in directing this effort will bless and enrich the lives of many who would not otherwise have the opportunity to move forward in educational or vocational pursuits."

The next step was to prepare for that board meeting. I found out from those who prepare the agenda for the Church Board of Education what the protocol is for meetings over which the First Presidency presides. Materials are placed in loose-leaf notebooks with an agenda at the back of the book. The books for each board member were to be delivered before the weekend of the meeting week. This gives the board members a chance to read and reflect on the materials before them. Since there was no precedent for this completely new department and board, I was prayerful and felt inspiration as I prepared. I wanted to give the board some idea of the scope of the problem we were addressing.

To do this I collected statistics from CES and the Missionary Department on numbers of institute students in countries and numbers of missionaries serving missions from various countries of the world. I also wanted to give them some of the history of the Perpetual Emigrating Company and fund. The Family and Church History Department was most helpful in gathering information for me. I had served two terms as executive director of that department and knew the people well. They provided me, among other things, with a copy of the original Perpetual Emigrating Company Articles of Incorporation filed in 1850 with the provisional State of Deseret. CES secretaries helped me prepare the notebooks and contents, and I delivered the binders to board members on Friday, 20 April. This accomplished, I flew off to Edmonton, Alberta, Canada to preside at a stake conference.

Another piece of the organizational puzzle fell into place on Monday, 23 April, after my return from Edmonton. On that day

I was able to attend the board meeting of a private foundation that had been making loans much as PEF would eventually do. Reed Dame, an old friend of mine and a former stake president from Oregon, presided over this board.

At that meeting I ran into Rex J. Allen, who had been released a little over a year earlier from presiding over the Switzerland Geneva Mission. He was an active member of that board. A Ph.D., Rex and his brother had developed a company that trained executives and employees for large corporations. Eventually they had sold that company then spent several years prior to Rex's call as mission president working as consultants to the new owners. Now he was free to use his tremendous talents in volunteer work. I asked him to come in to discuss PEF. Then, satisfied with his interest and availability, I obtained permission to invite him to serve with Chad and me as a volunteer director. I told him I would like to use about half of his time. As it turned out, he ended up working more than full-time, without salary. He has been invaluable in developing training materials, interfacing with departments, creating evaluation methods, and training those needing to implement PEF. He also, in concert with Russ Holt of the audio-visual department, quickly and inexpensively developed a brilliant video that introduces PEF to people. The pieces of the puzzle were beginning to come together.

Again, events leading up to Rex's deep involvement in PEF and his feelings for this initiative are best understood by reading his own words.

"What now?" "Where to from here?" These questions tolled in our hearts like Swiss church bells on a

Sunday morning. Nancy and I, with four of our seven children, were exhausted and stunned. Our mission was actually over, and as many before us, we were returning to a different world. We had carefully drawn a curtain on this day, July 1, 2000, and for three years we had not looked beyond. Now, questions long repressed in favor of "focus" loomed large. Friends? School? Aging parents? A new profession? Habitually, we muttered our family motto in rhythm with our hearts—"faith in every footstep, faith in every footstep. . . ."

Through the next months, the clouds and fatigue began to lift and some answers became clear. Yet much of what I pursued professionally seemed of little meaning. How could I continue to "make a significant difference?" For years, Nancy and I had carefully read the letters of our three older sons serving missions in South America. We were drawn to the plight of their native companions—intelligent, faithful, hardworking young men who could lead entire missions. Yet they often returned home to deep poverty and crushing discouragement. Could we help these great young people?

We scouted for others who were helping the poor. Some offered micro-credit loans and business training. Others offered medical or other resources, as well as hands-on volunteer service. Still others helped establish community cooperatives. All these were needed and noble efforts. Our hearts, however, still led us to focus whatever talent and resources we could muster to help "native" returned missionaries. We did not know how, but we felt impressed to try.

On 20 October 2000, in anticipation of my 46th birthday, I spent the morning trying to translate my aims in this and other areas into formal goals. Once typed, I taped them to my desk. One read as follows: "By December 2005, help to plan, design and successfully implement a self-perpetuating system that provides all 'native' returned missionaries the opportunity, via work and/or education, to become self-sufficient and able to effectively serve in the kingdom; this system must be built upon true principles, including Church Welfare principles."

In the next days, I crafted the skeleton of a plan that might fulfill this goal, wrestling with the great need to build self-reliance into the effort. Plus, it had to focus on education and training and it had to involve loans—a handout in any form could be worse than no help at all. And the whole Church organization would need to help.

With little to lose, I began to telephone acquaintances in various Church departments. Could I share some ideas and gather feedback? In mid-November, Bryan Weston, then a leader in the Church Educational System (CES), was kind enough to listen. He explained that CES had a limited program to provide educational loans to returned missionaries and other youth in developing countries. The results, he shared frankly, were mixed. He was encouraged by my little plan, however, and introduced me to Terry Oakes, then director of Employment Services in the welfare department, and his colleague, Chad Evans, who worked as a full-time volunteer to establish employment offices around the world. I had no idea at the time how important these men would become for me. They, too, were receptive to my plan, and I was allowed to attend an interdepartmental meeting in early December to discuss education and work opportunities for native returned missionaries. I learned for the first time that President Gordon B. Hinckley had long been intensely interested in this very issue. I was excited by these ideas and by the potential of that group, and I offered to help. They said they would call.

Then the wind shifted. Within a week I received a telephone message that there would be no further meetings at Church headquarters on this issue. I was thanked for my interest. That was it. It was only much later that I would learn why.

The months passed. Nancy and I pursued other ventures and did our best to serve. Then, with the rest of the Church, I was electrified on the evening of 31 March 2001 to hear President Hinckley proclaim the creation of the Church's Perpetual Education Fund. The announcement was made during the priesthood session of general conference.

Sitting with our sons in our stake center, I recall vividly how each sentence of this "constitutional" message entered my heart as fire. It poured over and through me in waves. And I was not alone in my tears as I glanced about the room.

It was, of course, the perfect answer—an elegant, sweeping, simple solution with a powerful historical precedent—far superior to any plan I had heard or conceived. It was not a "program," in the transitory sense, but a "bold initiative . . . inspired of the Lord." "Education," President Hinckley declared, was "the key to opportunity." Loans would be made to ambitious young men and women and the money would be repaid. They would attend local schools and train in vocations needed where they live. There would be no handouts—but an offering of opportunity. The existing Church organization would be tapped, including priesthood leaders and CES. There would be a small, new, independent department of the Church, staffed primarily by volunteers, to organize and coordinate the effort. A fund corpus would be established to generate income perpetually, from which the loans would be provided. Loan repayment would further perpetuate and increase the potential. Thousands would be blessed in many ways. Our prophet taught us that "we have a solemn obligation, a certain responsibility" to help, to lift, to participate. And he prayed for its success and for our involvement.

No words can describe how I felt. I knew once again that there is a prophet in Israel, and that a seer and a revelator was leading us. We rushed home to share this historic announcement with Nancy, our daughter Angela, and our beloved daughters-in-law. While we realized that we would not be directly involved in the dream that was so dear to us, we were grateful beyond expression. And for our sons' worthy companions in Peru, Chile, Bolivia, and elsewhere, we felt deep joy. It was right, and it would happen.

Still floating two days later, we learned that President Hinckley had called Elder John K. Carmack of the Seventy to serve as managing director of the new Perpetual Education Fund (PEF) department and to inaugurate and lead this great effort. Again, Nancy and I rejoiced. This talented, caring leader had served as our "first contact" in the Europe West Area presidency as we completed our mission in France and Switzerland. He had blessed us with his wisdom, experience, intelligence, and personal interest during our last year. What a teacher he was—warm, honest, and unpretentious, yet powerfully motivating. We had basked in his special witness of the Savior, and now we felt an added witness that with his leadership, the prophet's vision would be fully realized. We prayed fervently for his success, but never expected to meet him again.

It was something of a shock, then, when Elder

Carmack found me on my cell phone some two weeks later. Could I meet with him for a few minutes? We were perplexed. He knew nothing of our goals and our dreams—our commitment some six months before to somehow help native returned missionaries. He knew only vaguely of my skills and experience. And he knew nothing of my former brief encounter with Chad Evans, a volunteer in the Welfare Department. Yet when I appeared for the interview, there was Chad! And after only a brief interaction, we were both asked if we would become his "assistants" or "directors" in the new department. Could we donate 20 to 25 hours a week to help him work out the organization, processes, operations, training, financial concerns, and all else that would be needed to fulfill the prophetic vision?

I was stunned, of course, and overwhelmed. But there was only one answer. We began in earnest on 1 May 2001, and we soon realized those 25 hours per week would extend to 60 or 70 or more. We simply dropped everything else. President Hinckley was more than earnest about our progress. He spoke with Elder Carmack regularly and met monthly with us and with the new PEF board of directors. *Had we made any loans?* He wanted results. Indeed, in our first meeting, President Hinckley eyed Chad and me carefully. Then he turned to Elder Carmack: "John, work these men to death!" Was it a sentence or a blessing?

Others were interested as well, and we met with President Boyd K. Packer, the entire Quorum of the Twelve, the presidents of the Seventy, and other committees and groups. The pace was intense. Elder Carmack worked from a borrowed office, while Chad and I shared a small converted file room crammed with two secondhand desks and folding chairs. We used our own computers, printers, and paper and went to work—now a three-person department. While we discussed everything together, and prayed in unity for guidance, roles naturally emerged. Elder Carmack provided oversight and direction, of course, while Chad focused on operations and finance, and I emphasized training and communications. By August, Elder Richard E. Cook joined our team to apply his wide experience in international finance.

President Hinckley's inaugural speech became our constitution, by-laws, and plan for operations and training. We pored over it dozens of times, gaining insight as we grew. With essentially no budget, we built a short inspirational film that combined the prophet's address with stories from the field. We created processes and policies and training materials in multiple languages. We drew heavily on the time and expertise of leaders in CES and other departments affected by PEF. Certainly, that summer we must have seemed something of a whirlwind in the middle of the Church organization and its standard procedures. Still, people were generally patient and helpful, and in under four months, slightly ahead of President Hinckley's initial promise to begin in the fall of 2001, we were ready to visit the first three areas and to test our initial approach.

In the meantime, we had begun as soon as possible to involve those in the field—first in Peru, Mexico, and Chile—in our planning and development. President Hinckley's address had stirred intense interest among millions of Church members and leaders everywhere. When will *we* have access to the loans? What are the criteria? Why not *here* first? Our board of directors took charge of the rollout schedule and locations and encouraged us to be wise in our haste. With their immense experience, they sensed the difficulties and complexities that are inherent in working with multiple cultures, languages, laws, customs, and educational systems.

Our first field trips in August and September helped us significantly improve processes, training, and organization. The principles and practices outlined in President Hinckley's address and in our board meetings proved to be the "polar star" to which we always returned. General Authorities in the various areas provided excellent input, as well as the youth and their leaders. Everyone willingly spent many extra hours to begin training and implementation.

By late September 2001, we approved the first

PEF loans, and ambitious young people began to catch hold of this "bright ray of hope," as President Hinckley would describe it. Stories of prayers answered and blessings fulfilled began rolling in. We met the youth in their homes and in the institutes. We wept together and worked together. They taught us much of sacrifice and faith. They put up with our mistakes and missteps. We helped them to see a new vision of hope, achievement, and success in work, family, and the Church.

As I now write this in the summer of 2003, the PEF story continues to evolve daily, and there are yet hurdles to cross and challenges to resolve. We have approved nearly 10,000 loans and many recipients have graduated from their training programs to reap the benefits foreseen by the prophet. It has been a great privilege for me and for Nancy and our family to be involved. We had no idea that a goal made in secret would be thus openly rewarded, and we only pray we have helped and not hurt this "bold initiative." The Perpetual Education Fund is critical to the progress of the Kingdom of God on earth. It is indeed a "bright ray of hope," a shining example of our Lord's love for all, His mercy, and His justice. It is essential for our remarkable young brothers and sisters across the world. It provides vision, hope, and real opportunity and growth toward independence. Participants will become sorely needed leaders and examples of gospel abundance. It is a rare and

> needed opportunity for us to learn sacrifice and con-
> secration. It is a step toward real reconciliation, and
> a reflection of the infinite atonement. We pray it will
> go forward to fulfill its prophetic vision.

Wednesday, 25 April 2001, was an historic day. We held our first board meeting, chaired by President Hinckley. The entire First Presidency, Elder M. Russell Ballard, Elder Henry B. Eyring, Bishop H. David Burton (Presiding Bishop of the Church), Sister Mary Ellen W. Smoot (Relief Society General President), Elder L. Aldin Porter (Senior President of the Seventy), Stan Peterson, and Brook Hales (PEF board secretary) attended the meeting in the board room of the First Presidency. We discussed the future of PEF and the way to proceed to bring it about. The board, and particularly President Hinckley, gave us good direction. President Hinckley assigned me to prepare articles of organization, by-laws to operate the department, and legal instruments to be used in the loan process. He asked that I bring all of these documents and other items necessary to establish the department and program of operation to the next board meeting in May. This was a pivotal day in my new assignment, and I felt the load of the world on my shoulders by the conclusion of the meeting. Nevertheless, I felt both the potential greatness of PEF, as well as its burdens.

On the weekend following the meeting, I went to Seattle to preside at a stake conference. On my return I spent the last Monday of this busy April thinking through the policies and documents necessary to administer PEF. Inspiration flowed generously, comforting me. By the end of the day I had written the first draft of the articles, policies, and supporting documents needed to implement President Hinckley's vision of what needed to be done. I had spent the entire day alone, thinking, writing, and working on these matters and felt the inspiration of the Lord in the process.

During the month of April, Shirley and I were adjusting to being home, launching a new program into orbit, taking up domestic General Authority duties, and reacquainting ourselves with our family. Although we have agreed that we would not want to repeat such a month, we felt happy and satisfied that we were going to succeed with the help of the Lord. We felt that nothing we might have been doing could compare in importance with what we were now shouldering. It seemed that the Lord was with us in almost every small and seemingly inconsequential matter that arose in connection with PEF.

By the first of May we had a team working together to create the program of PEF. The Presiding Bishopric and Brother Harold Brown made available the services of Chad Evans, and Rex Allen had agreed to come to work on a part-time basis. The three of us met on 1 May to share ideas and responsibilities. We formed almost a presidency of PEF.

Whenever I saw President Hinckley, I found him vitally interested in what we were doing. The pressure to get the program rolling was enormous. We were in the development phase of the project, grappling with questions such as what criteria to use for granting loans, how to disperse the fund, how to help applicants get the kind of career training they needed, how to collect repayments, and who would take responsibility for each aspect of the work. I talked with Church Treasury Services about the process of operating a near global banking system to handle disbursements and collections. We also wanted to add a unified and artistic flavor to our applications, documents, and training materials. Everywhere we turned, people had ideas for us to consider and conveyed generous offers to help. Sadly, we couldn't use most of them, but we have appreciated every good desire to help.

Other assignments continued for Shirley and me. Some were away from Utah. While we were away from the office on these assignments, the world had crashed in on the secretaries in the CES office. Many calls had come in about various matters concerning PEF. They were busy all day Monday, 7 May, answering inquiries. They could not answer most of the questions, and this work was not part of their job. But this constant interest in PEF portended the effect the program would have on the Church. It was impacting many Church employees and exciting thousands. No one complained, but many felt the heat. There was little I could do except empathize with them and share with them that I, too, was feeling the pressure.

We also began to administer the International Education Fund mentioned above and took responsibility for about a dozen other loan and grant programs at the same time. The pressures were mounting. Fortunately, although the complexity of our work was growing, Chad and Rex were proving innovative and powerful assistants. Still, even with their help, I went home at night wondering how we were going to accomplish all that was expected of us.

By 9 May, I felt that the PEF team was gelling. That day we met with the International Employment Coordinating Committee, chaired by Harold Brown. Serving on this committee were representatives from Welfare Services, CES, BYU, Ricks

College (now BYU–Idaho), LDS Business College, the Priesthood Department, and others. We could see that our work impacted all of them in one way or another.

We were getting closer to having the documents prepared for the board meeting in late May. Rex and Chad were working in tandem on the procedures for granting, disbursing, and collecting PEF loans. I was working on a schedule for the rollout of the program. Our goal was to have the essential program and documents completed and ready by Friday, 18 May, well ahead of our deadline for delivering to the board agenda and papers. It was a tall order, but we were confident we could do it. Many other things vied for our attention, but we kept at our central task, coordinating our work in presidency-type meetings. By Thursday, 17 May, we had our program ready with the help of Janis. Rex and Chad had literally worked night and day on the structure of the work. We revised the documents over and over and finally had something ready to present, including a reworking of my original loan application draft.

Friends and strangers continued to send in small and large contributions, and the fund was growing daily, giving us hope that it would one day be sufficiently large to do what President Hinckley and the Lord had in mind for it to do. On Friday, 18 May, our self-imposed deadline to have the program in condition to present to the board, we met to put finishing touches on the paper work. On that day, a young married sister, who left no name or address, dropped off a small wrapped package at my office as a gift to PEF. I opened it and found she had left a two-karat diamond ring, her own wedding ring, with a note that she and her husband had decided together to donate it to the fund. We felt even more humble in the face of such a demonstration of love. This program had obviously reached into the hearts of literally hundreds of thousands. By the close of the day we were ready to meet the board well ahead of schedule.

Over the weekend I presided at a stake conference in Idaho Falls, among friends I had made while serving as mission president in Idaho. On returning, I worked with my journals to prepare the talk I would give to the Seventy as my term of service expired. This was scheduled for Thursday, 24 May, during the regular meetings of the Quorums of Seventy. On Tuesday of that week, Rex, Chad, and I went over our program for presentation to the board of directors. Rex, a master at presentations, prepared a major part of it. On Wednesday, I met with the Church budget director, Craig Christensen, who helped prepare a department budget to present to the board for the balance of the year 2001. The Church agreed to pay all expenses of operating this program out of the budget so that 100 percent of the donated funds could go for the central purpose of PEF: to make needed loans for the training and education of returned missionaries and others in less-advantaged countries. Contributions continued to flow into the fund from every direction. McClain Bybee, managing director of the LDS Foundation, which coordinates fund raising for Church schools and other causes, came by to talk things over and pledge Foundation support in the development of PEF.

Since Elder Henry B. Eyring was the Commissioner of Education for the Church, I thought it important to review with him the documents to be presented to the board ahead of the meeting. I did this on Friday, 25 May. He seemed pleased with our work and gave some good suggestions. I told Chad and Rex to take the entire Memorial Day weekend off, away from PEF and with their families. They had worked constantly for the fund since coming aboard and had done a great job. Offers from other volunteers continued to roll in, some of them very insistent that they be given the opportunity to serve. If only we could have used every one of them, we would have been pleased to do so. That weekend a close friend and his wife dropped by our home with a very large donation for the fund. Their generosity was deeply touching.

The day before the 29 May board meeting, I met President Hinckley on my way to lunch. He asked me how many loans we had made. I thought how like him it was to want the program up and running, making loans, even before the board had approved our plans. He was always way ahead of us in his thinking. In the afternoon we held a dry run for the board presentation we would make the next day. It became evident once again that these faithful brethren working with me were great and energetic young men. We also discovered that the fund had doubled over the amount reported at the last board meeting.

On Wednesday, 30 May, we made our presentation to the board. I also worked on finishing touches for my presentation to the Quorums of Seventy the next day. We had early technical problems with the computer for our presentation to the board, a common occurrence in life, but Rex was up to the task of making things work. I had invited Chad and Rex to attend the board meeting and participate in the presentation so that the board could get acquainted with them. President Hinckley and the board approved the program we presented in every detail, and then President Hinckley made it clear he wanted this program up and running as soon as possible. But after pushing us to the limit, he complimented us on the work we had done in fleshing out the program. The board members also seemed pleased with our progress.

I told the board that I wanted and needed one additional director to work with us, someone who had experience in international finance, such as Elder Richard E. Cook, who was serving in the Asia Area presidency but would be coming home from Hong Kong that summer. On hearing that suggestion, President Hinckley said: "We all know Richard; those in favor, say 'Aye.'" Thus was Richard Cook, who had yet to learn about what he might do during this part of his retirement, selected and approved for his calling. Following his spontaneous appointment, it happened that Richard had a question to ask me on behalf of his area presidency. And so he called me by telephone at home. It also happened that I had some questions for him, and soon he was looking forward to a new assignment for which he was exceptionally well qualified. But let's hear Richard's story in his own words.

In the spring of 2001, Mary and I traveled home from Hong Kong to attend general conference. Our assignment was to the Asia Area. The Asia Area office is in Hong Kong where I was a counselor to Elder Cree-L Kofford.

I was sitting with the other General Authorities in the general priesthood meeting when President Hinckley made the historic announcement establishing the Perpetual Education Fund. Like it was for most members of the Church, that announcement was thrilling to me, and I knew immediately that I was witnessing an historic moment. Most of the twenty-three nations in the Asia Area are third-world countries, and I knew these countries would be eventual beneficiaries of this inspired program.

Aside from the program coming from our prophet, I knew it made sense, was timely, and from my efforts to establish a Mongolian Education Endowment Fund I knew that it was needed to build the kingdom. Furthermore, I had a very strong feeling that somehow, someway, I would be involved in the program. In some respects, I hesitate to share this feeling that I would be involved because, since joining the PEF organization, I've had many people call and volunteer their services, telling me that they have had a similar feeling. Unfortunately, to date, we have not been able to use all of them. On the other hand, everyone in the Church can participate in PEF without joining the working organization.

Following general conference, my wife and I traveled back to Hong Kong and our work, but my feelings about PEF persisted. These feelings were fed somewhat by Elder Kofford saying to me one day, knowing I would be released as a Seventy in October 2001: "Richard, you could make a great contribution to the PEF program."

I knew Elder Carmack well. When Sister Cook and I were called as missionaries to Mongolia, Elder

Carmack had been the area president and had made several trips to Mongolia.

One day, I think it was in May, I had a reason to call Elder Carmack about some issue or another. I can't recall now exactly what it was, but Elder Carmack had spent four years in the Asia Area, and from time to time we had historical questions that only members of former presidencies could answer.

As I thought about calling Elder Carmack, I had a strong impression that he would say something about my involvement in the PEF program. As expected, when we had completed our conversation on the other matter, John said: "Richard, I'm going to suggest to the First Presidency that you join us to help with the financial aspects of PEF. How would you feel about that?" It was then that I had the full realization that indeed the Spirit had been confirming that my new assignment would be with PEF. A few days later, Elder Carmack called back and reported that the PEF board of directors had approved my participation in the program. Elder Carmack told me that in the board meeting he had said: "We need someone working with us that has a heavy finance background, someone like Elder Cook who is returning this summer from Asia." Whereupon, without further discussion, President Hinckley is reported to have said: "Are there any objections to calling Elder Cook to join the PEF program?" There were none, and I began serving in August of 2001.

On the last day of May, I addressed the Seventy assembled in quorum meeting. It is traditional that outgoing Seventy are invited to express their feelings at that momentous time in their lives. I spoke from notes and shared sacred things with my brethren.

In the afternoon, with the help of Rex and Chad, I presented our program to the CES zone administrators and others from the CES. They had lots of questions and suggestions. We were now ready to try out the program by training those who would have the responsibility to lead out in part of Latin America. The board had approved our suggestion that we start the program in Peru, Chile, and Mexico. As May ended, I realized how busy it had been and how far we had come. My confidence that we would be able to fulfill our assignment grew daily.

Elder M. Russell Ballard called on the first of June, requesting that we make a presentation about PEF to the Quorum of the Twelve on Tuesday morning, 5 June. I considered that a very important invitation because we needed every member of the Twelve to know and feel that we were being true to the vision of the First Presidency and Quorum of the Twelve. Rex, Chad, and I went to work on our presentation. The Area Committee, a high level committee that looks after all of the areas of the Church, also asked that we present the program to their committee, informing them of the progress we had made. That presentation was scheduled for Wednesday, 6 June. Since I had personal business in Boston, it would be up to Rex and Chad to prepare the presentations; both went smoothly. President Boyd K. Packer made some excellent suggestions for improving how we presented it. We took his suggestions to heart.

We now began the responsibility of administering the IEF in place of CES. Stan Peterson of CES spent much time with me going over the details of the past administration and pledged help from CES. After meeting with Stan we presented the program to the Area Committee. Committee members decided that rather than hearing and seeing our prepared presentation, they would like to ask questions and find out what was really happening with PEF in an informal give-and-take session. They had good suggestions and seemed to resonate with us in the direction they perceived the fund was moving.

Tatiana and Maylin, Peru

These two sisters came from a very poor home. When their father could no longer support them as teen-agers, he prayed fervently and sent them alone to make their way in Lima. Then, when PEF was offered, they each determined to enter school. They have since become leaders in their programs—nursing and medical technology.

These youth join thousands worldwide who now *press forward* with hope, courage, and faith—fulfilling prophetic promises.

CHAPTER SIX

MOVING THE FOCUS OUTWARD

*Effective executives focus on
outward contribution. They gear their efforts
to results rather than to work.*

PETER F. DRUCKER, *THE EFFECTIVE EXECUTIVE*, 24

THUS FAR, OF NECESSITY, we had concentrated on building a team and creating the PEF program. But none of this had provided either career guidance or loan assistance to a single young person. It was time to stop focusing on the internal workings of the system and turn our efforts outward.

We spent Monday, 11 June, preparing for our first field visit, aware that during these first forays abroad we would be learning as much as training. The day was chaotic and busy, but we worked through our plans and felt ready to go. In the afternoon I gave an interview to the *Ensign* on behalf of PEF. We departed early on 12 June for our trip. We decided to go first as a team to Mexico, Peru, and Chile, to meet some of those who would have to carry on the program in the field. Rex, Chad, and Bryan Weston of CES traveled with me. Chad had made many of the preparations, knowing as he did many of the key Church employees in these countries from his work with Church employment. This was historic and exciting.

After arriving in Lima, Peru, we met with the area presidency, Elders Ned Roueche, David Stone, and Juan Uceda. In the afternoon we visited SENATI, an impressive technical school that trains students for fifty occupations, ranging from mechanical work to textiles. We were told that they had a total of 180,000 students enrolled in their several locations. At another school we observed young people being trained in brick laying, architecture design, computer operations, electrical installation, plumbing, and other trades. Yet another school we visited offered training in telecommunications and how to produce training videos. This school also offered courses in fiber optics. We were reassured to find that outstanding schools emphasizing vocational training were available to our young people.

On 13 June, we met with about 100 institute of religion students, mostly returned missionaries. We shared background about the fund and answered questions. Revealingly, the first question asked was, "How can we contribute to the fund?" Most of those present signified that they would need and want loans to help them gain training and education. Many were married, and a number were over thirty years of age, still trying to find a way to improve their employment skills.

We continued visiting schools the next day and also visited a government-associated student loan organization. The managers there shared their procedures and business know-how with us. They offered to become the organization that would be our loan collectors in Peru.

That afternoon we flew to Santiago, Chile, where we met with

Elders Dale Miller and Stephen Oveson of the Chile Area area presidency and Robert Driggs, who had just arrived in Chile with his wife, Gay, and who would serve as executive secretary to the presidency. Later that day we were pleased to see Elder Robert E. Wells and his wife, Helen, who were presiding in the Santiago Temple. Elder John A. Harris, the third member of the area presidency, who was not in attendance at the first meeting, joined us.

In the afternoon we enjoyed an in-depth visit with Óscar A. Marín Castello of the Banco del Desarrollo, the bank that administers about 80% of the student loans in Chile. By practicing strict control, the bank had a high collection rate for their loans, and Mr. Castello indicated they would be pleased to manage our loans for a reasonable fee. Their success was due in part to a policy that borrowers begin immediately making small payments on their loans. We later adopted that same policy for PEF. We were learning as we traveled. Again, we spoke to a group of returned missionaries at an institute of religion gathering.

While in Santiago, we visited with the treasurer of the Chile chapter of the Missionary Education Fund, the private foundation Rex had been associated with when he joined the PEF team. We learned much about their program of making loans to returned missionaries. On a small scale, they were trying to do for Chile what we were going to do globally. (Eventually PEF would absorb that admirable program.)

We then flew to Mexico City to repeat the training for leaders there and to learn all we could in the process. We were nearing completion of our three-country trip. Looking back, we realized how far we still had to go to iron out difficulties, put procedures in place, and address concerns; but we had done the best we knew how up to that point. In Mexico City we met with the Mexico South area presidency, Elders Carl B. Pratt, Richard H. Winkel, and Armando Gaona. We trained, learned, shared, and visited Church and CES facilities and vocational schools. On Sunday we attended Church, visited the MTC, toured the visitors' center presided over by the Bluths, old friends, and finally held our own meeting with just the four of us who had taken this training and exploratory trip. We reviewed what we had learned on this initial trip. During our final day in Mexico, we again visited schools, including the famed Benemérito School that is owned and administered by the Church. We toured vocational and technical schools and met government officials who administer the huge loan programs available to students in Mexico.

By the end of our tour, we felt that PEF was now on its way. If we had known then how far we yet had to go, we might have been discouraged, but our spirits were high. This was going to work!

Back at Church headquarters in Salt Lake City, we continued to receive much attention and were showered with invitations and opportunities to speak about PEF. Duties in my calling as a Seventy continued through the rest of the month. President Hinckley celebrated his 91st birthday on Friday, 22 June. Gifts and messages of congratulation poured in. General Authorities were invited to a party in his honor at noon. His mind was obviously still focused on PEF because he called me that afternoon, wanting to know what we had found on our Latin American trip. He seemed delighted with my brief report. Things were moving, and he could relax a little on a matter that obviously was weighing heavily on his mind.

I attended a stake conference in Colorado, my last stake

conference as a General Authority. Arriving home after the conference, Shirley and I suddenly realized how tired we were and what an intense three months we had experienced. We were amazed at the progress the program had made and the doors that had opened. We knew the source behind the progress. In no way did we deserve the credit for it.

Life went on for all of us. Rex's mother had heart surgery, funerals for friends came and went, close associates married, and two new grandchildren arrived in our family. All of this happened in the background of overriding responsibility. Little by little, PEF began to manage other funds that various members had created for worthy and related purposes. We worked on brochures to share with applicants and interested parties. Rex took on that project after I had worked out a draft and received suggestions from our son-in-law Erik Jacobsen, who is in the graphics design business. My first draft was left on the cutting floor, and a much better brochure emerged under Rex's able hand. Good men and women continued to drop in with generous donations to the fund, some of which were sizeable, all of which came unannounced and unadvertised. We turned our minds to the second half of this start-up year. President Hinckley allowed us to have one paid employee, a secretary. And so on Friday, 29 June, Debbie Muir became our department secretary. Later, Catherine Wenschlag, one of the sisters who worked on the IEF and Wilkinson Loan Funds as an accounting clerk, was transferred from CES to our department. Finance also transferred Brent Plowman to our department as the department controller. Neither really added to the Church payroll because they were transferred, not hired as new, full-time employees.

The July break was now on us. No stake conferences were scheduled in July. If a General Authority desires a vacation and can arrange his affairs to the purpose, July is the month to do it. We looked back with wonder on the 11 February telephone call in Frankfurt that had changed our lives once again.

We worked in more family time but continued to work on PEF throughout July. I had wanted to do some historical research on related topics and used the University of Utah library during the month to good advantage. Rex and Chad continued their diligent service, working on the nuts and bolts of the program. We also found other volunteers to assist in the work. Berkley Spencer, an expert in welfare and humanitarian matters and a BYU professor who had lived many years in Latin America, joined us from time to time to share his understanding of those countries. He had worked as a CES area director in Central America, had helped establish employment centers for the Welfare Department, and had also served as a mission president in Chile. His background was rich indeed. Offers to help beyond what we could use continued to flow in.

I needed some time to write assigned articles and to prepare talks about the new program. With PEF such a hot topic, my speaking schedule was unusually full. Almost every trip resulted in a chance meeting with someone who wanted to contribute and help with the program. The month of July provided a needed chance to think and do research. I enjoyed it very much and felt better prepared to address problems we faced when the month ended.

On 26 July, a group from the Westminster 3rd Ward of the Huntington Beach California North Stake brought us a sizeable check for PEF. It seems that they had a surplus after paying the expenses of their youth conference. We were grateful for the generosity of the youth and their leaders.

Rex had continued to work on a motivational video that we could use to introduce the program. The Church audio-visual department produced the film, essentially without a separate budget. Rex wrote the script, and Russ Holt did the professional work with the help of the department staff. The video featured President Hinckley's opening address and footage shot in Latin America. Several of us gave brief interviews for Russ to use. The film turned out well and was thereafter most useful in bringing to viewers the spirit of PEF.

Enterprise Mentors International—a private foundation that included such luminaries in its leadership as Elder Marion D. Hanks, Menlo Smith, Ray Barnes, Richard Headlee, Dick Oscarson, and others—invited the PEF team to share our work and progress with their board of directors. We enjoyed meeting with them in early August to learn about their outstanding humanitarian efforts in less-advantaged countries, which in some ways paralleled our own beginning work. We explained to them, as we had to others, that PEF was not meant to supplant or supersede their program or the many others that are doing such great things to help humanity. Rather, we had an important but specific role to play and hoped to cooperate with them in their work. Some organizations, watching the formation of PEF, felt a bit confused and concerned by our entrance into a field that they had occupied. As we explained our role to such people, the concern and confusion usually left.

Because the PEF would affect virtually all of the Seventy,

especially when assigned overseas, we met on 7 August with those
leaving shortly for their area presidency callings in foreign countries. We shared with them the essentials of the program and
answered questions. All were vitally interested and supportive. The
next day I met privately with President Hinckley who continued
to be both excited about our efforts and concerned that PEF
quickly take its place in the Church. He gave excellent counsel. It
continued to amaze us that he could keep so many matters in his
mind and even more that he cared so much about what we were
doing. He was visibly delighted with the progress, but urged us on
in the work of making his vision a reality. My associates, Rex and
Chad, left for another trip to Latin America on 9 August to continue the work of perfecting the mechanisms of PEF in South
America and Mexico. Our outward focus intensified.

An interesting incident showing the magnetism of the PEF
concept in the lives of people occurred on 13 August. I had lunch
with two large donors to the fund. One of them had had a chance
meeting with Gardner H. Russell, a former colleague in the seventy, who, on meeting our donor, challenged him on the spot and
at their first meeting to donate $100,000 to PEF just about the
time President Hinckley was introducing it to the priesthood. The
donor accepted the challenge and made the large donation on the
strength of a chance meeting with a new friend. Such was the
power of the PEF concept in the lives of many.

When President Hinckley called me in Frankfurt on 11
February, he requested that I serve as managing director of PEF as
a General Authority until I was given emeritus status and to continue serving thereafter as a volunteer. On 14 August, I completed
my last assignment as an active seventy. The formal conferral of

emeritus status would await the October 2001 semiannual conference, but my official work was then complete. To reach the end of such an intense period of activity brought a strange feeling, but the next day, a day I described in my journal as the first day of the rest of our lives, was just as busy as the prior ones. Church members, of both humble and substantial means, continued to drop by to offer support and learn more about our work.

I kept the road between Salt Lake City and Provo busy as I gave talks to various groups that were meeting on the BYU campus. For example, I taught several classes at the request of faculty friends. Rex and Chad cut short vacations to help me prepare for various important presentations such as the August board meeting. While updating PEF documents for the upcoming meeting, we received the great news that the first twenty applications for loans from PEF had come in. That was an exciting and historic moment. The day before the next board meeting, a Tuesday, we received a few more applications. We also met that day with Wesley Jones, the Church auditor, to talk over auditing and process questions.

The board meeting brought with it strong counsel and direction. Such counsel always made us feel even more keenly the importance of our assignment and also helped us give credit to the proper source of our help. Life continued to be busy and interesting as August came to a close. We were getting closer to making President Hinckley's vision a reality, but we all felt the pressure of doing it right and getting it done. September loomed as a critical month.

Richard Cook, who had joined the PEF team in August, chaired the first loan committee meeting on Tuesday, 4 September.

It was a charter day as we considered the first 35 applications for PEF loans. We gave it the closest concentration and greatest spiritual effort we could muster. We wanted so much to be in harmony with the goals of the program and to do it right.

The next day we left for northern Mexico to introduce the program to the Mexico North Area. We trained the area presidency, CES, welfare, finance, and other leaders. Elder Lynn A. Mickelsen, the area president, and his wife, Jeanine, hosted us in their home. While there, Bill and Vicky Treu, old friends assigned to oversee temple construction, showed us the as-yet-unfinished Monterrey Mexico Temple. An idea that has become a cornerstone of our in-field organization was hatched in Monterrey when Elder Mickelsen suggested that the area presidency had to be in charge and directly involved. We agreed with him, and that became the catalyst for the creation in each area of an area PEF committee chaired by a member of the area presidency. The vice-chairman of the committee would be the area CES director. If an Employment Resource Center director was in place, he or she would serve on the committee together with the area controller, legal counsel, and director of Temporal Affairs. This new concept, born in Mexico, has been absolutely critical to the success of our work.

I left on Saturday, 8 September, for Brazil, traveling alone. Little did I know what would befall the United States during that trip. Arriving in São Paulo on Sunday, 9 September, I was joined at the airport by Oswaldo Bossi, who became my traveling companion for the Brazil trip. We continued right on to Recife in the northern part of Brazil where Elder Robert S. Wood, the area president, and Elder Darwin B. Christenson, his counselor, met us. After a shower and shave, we jumped immediately into our training of the leaders in the Brazil North Area and were able to clear up many misconceptions about PEF. The area presidency supported our efforts beautifully. We met a packed stake center of returned missionaries and other young adults. They came to learn about PEF. After two days and a night without decent sleep, I was ready to fall into a bed at 11:00 P.M. that night. We continued with training meetings and a visit to the Recife Brazil Temple the next day. In the afternoon, Elder Robert R. Steuer of the area presidency accompanied us to Fortaleza by airplane where we duplicated the training and met with another large group of interested young people in an informative fireside. I explained the history and policy of PEF and met with the stake presidents in the area. That night I had a fitful sleep at best.

The next day was 11 September 2001, a date destined to join 7 December 1941 as a day of infamy. At an early breakfast we heard a sketchy report, one that proved inaccurate, that an airplane had accidentally flown into and damaged the Empire State Building. Next we heard that it was the World Trade Center that had been struck, and probably by terrorists. As we continued with our work we learned that airplanes had struck both World Trade Center towers and heard an additional erroneous report that a truck had blown up half of the Pentagon near Washington D.C. We then heard that a number of other hijacked airplanes were in the air with unknown targets. As the facts proved, two airplanes struck the World Trade Center towers and a third struck the Pentagon. A fourth crashed in Pennsylvania due to the intervention of heroic individuals aboard. We were horrified and shocked along with most of the world. Nevertheless, we continued our journey by flying from Fortaleza to Salvador, stopping at Recife en route.

At the Salvador Airport we saw on a television screen the horrifying footage of two airplanes crashing into the twin World Trade Center buildings. We continued to the chapel where we spent the rest of the day and night duplicating the training we had given in the other Brazil cities, keeping an eye on television to learn the awful truth of the day that changed life for so many of us. We continued to do our work with a heavy heart.

Mercifully, our work occupied our minds except between training meetings. Again we had a fireside for potential applicants for PEF loans. We flew back to Recife where Elder Wood picked us up. By then we knew of the gravity and extent of the terrorist attack. We knew that loss of lives had been in the thousands when we went to bed. The next day, 12 September, I attended a Brazil North Area presidency meeting and took much of the time in that meeting training them. We kept up with the news between meetings, but continued with our busy schedule. I wondered about my wife who was in Boston, where the two flights that crashed into the World Trade Center had originated. I knew that she was already there and didn't worry about her safety, but we all turned our thoughts to our families at that time of world crisis.

Starting 13 September, we began our training in the Brazil South Area with Elders Athos M. Amorim, Adhemar Damiani, and Neil L. Andersen of the area presidency. I stayed with Neil and Cathy Andersen in São Paulo. In addition to training all of the leaders, we visited occupational training schools, including a branch of SENATI. We saw students in training for such occupations as metallurgy, welding, electrical work, repair and operation of computers, construction work, and telecommunications. We visited other schools and held yet another fireside with the youth.

Flights to the United States were all canceled that week. I had no idea when I would be able to fly home, but we continued on to Curitiba in order to train CES leaders and stake presidents and speak with the youth. We had a wonderful time and the young people attending our firesides were enthusiastic. They came in large numbers everywhere we went. On Sunday night we had about 800 in our final fireside in São Paulo. We left directly for the airport from the fireside. My flight, leaving at midnight for Dallas, was the first flight to depart Brazil for the United States following the tragedy. We were late getting started, but the trip to Dallas was safe and I slept a bit during the night. Once in Texas, I had my first chance to call Shirley. She had indeed been in Boston on 11 September. Even for those of us not directly touched by the death and destruction of 11 September, the experience was harrowing. Soon I was home with Shirley after a magnificent and useful time working on PEF affairs.

The next night I spoke to members of the Cannon-Hinckley Club about PEF. The Cannon-Hinckley Club is an old and distinguished organization, stressing Church history. I included words of comfort and attempted to impart understanding of the horrible events of the past week. It was a sobering night of reflection for all.

Shirley and I visited my Aunt Blonda Yount in California on Saturday, 29 September. On the way home from our visit with Aunt Blonda, we sat next to a stranger on the plane who asked Shirley if she knew how to get in touch with the man in charge of PEF. That question was like lobbing a softball for us to hit. We enjoyed a great talk with a man who has become our friend. I knew his father well in the Whittier California Stake. Early the next week he brought a sizeable donation to our office. Everyone, it seemed, wanted to help make President Hinckley's great vision a reality. With the close of September 2001, six months had come and gone since PEF was introduced to the Church. They were exciting and difficult months. We felt that we had made substantial progress in launching the PEF program. I continued to feel a heavy burden of responsibility to make the prophet's vision a reality, but in many important respects it had already become a reality. We had made our first loans, had thought through and refined the basics of the program, and had begun testing it in several countries. Much remained to be done, but we were on our way. We hoped the first six months would prove to be the hardest. They were certainly the most creative. The fund itself had already become large, with tens of millions of dollars having been donated.

The semiannual general conference in October 2001 found us trying to take advantage of the presence of those international area presidencies who came home for training. Between the broadcasting of conference sessions on television, the stations broadcast the video introducing PEF. Thousands viewed it and learned about the new program. Many came by to greet us in our offices in the high-rise Church Office Building. Among the visitors were Steve and Betty Gibson from Provo, Utah. They had developed an academy for Filipino Saints in the Philippine Islands. Their plan was to give business development training to returned missionaries in the Philippines, providing them with the tools to start their own businesses. We talked over ways we could cooperate in our work. During general conference, the Church granted me emeritus status, along with several other colleagues. I didn't think this would bring much change in our lives, but as it played out, it relieved Shirley and me of tremendous time commitments and responsibilities, allowing us to concentrate on PEF.

During the formal training of the General Authorities, the Brethren gave me fifteen minutes to address all of our General Authority colleagues on the subject of PEF. We gave them a handout and a brief sketch of what we had accomplished since the introduction of the program by President Hinckley on 31 March. We felt their love and support in what had been delegated to us.

On Friday, 5 October, before general sessions began, the First Presidency honored those of us retiring from active work as General Authorities at a luncheon held in the Ambassador Room in the Joseph Smith Memorial Building. Those honored were men of the first quorum completing their active full-time service in the work and second quorum members completing their terms of service. Those of the first quorum were Elders L. Aldin Porter, Vaughn J. Featherstone, Rex D. Pinegar, L. Lionel Kendrick, and myself. Those of the second quorum were Elders Richard E. Cook, Wayne M. Hancock, Ray H. Wood, and Richard B. Wirthlin. President Hinckley made gracious remarks about the service we had rendered and presented each of us with a framed letter of release signed by the First Presidency. The week had been full of emotion and nostalgia, but more was ahead.

Conference sessions were wonderful. In the general priesthood meeting, President Hinckley made another substantial reference to our work, and mentioned those of us involved in making the PEF a reality, giving another tremendous boost to the program.

An amusing remark that would be referred to time and time again was that, having worn Elder Cook and Elder Carmack out on the front side, he was turning us over to wear us out on the back side. His remark was truer than he perhaps knew. If I thought Saturday was an emotional day, Sunday was even more so as bombing began and missiles were fired on targets in Afghanistan. President Hinckley referred to those events at the beginning of his afternoon address, as usual saying exactly the right things to set a proper tone for the meeting. He concluded the session with a unique public prayer. We relaxed at home that evening, knowing our service as a General Authority and wife had concluded.

With general conference over, we faced a busy telephone on Tuesday, 9 October. PEF was on the minds of many. We had our final social for the Seventy that evening. Although we felt relief, we also felt a bit hollow at the conclusion of a long and incredibly busy and packed period of our lives. An era had ended for us, an era we had loved, but one we were pleased to have completed. But, as President Howard Hunter taught the Church, one door closes and another opens.

People continued to offer to work full- or part-time without salary for PEF, and some offered other meaningful help, including the use of computer programs that could handle loan details. The staff and executive committee of PEF met to consider what we had learned during the weeks and months before general conference.

Suggestions for how we could and should operate came from all over. Had we tried to follow every idea, we never could have focused on our work; but those giving suggestions were trying to help and were sincere in their proffered advice.

On Friday, 19 October, we added a new set of missionaries to our staff. They were Gordon and Janice Creer. They quickly made themselves indispensable, handling the loan applications and helping perfect the technical processes of the headquarters functions as well as directly interfacing with the workers in the field who actually handle the applications and financial processes. Gordon had worked for Chrysler Motor Company, handling similar matters, and we quickly found he and Janice were not afraid of long hours. With the Creers aboard, we had a fairly full staff, able to handle most of the problems that arose day to day.

Rex continued to demonstrate the ability to keep dozens of projects going. He kept busy creating, revising, and simplifying training materials for PEF. Chad had the ability to stay positive and the initiative to make things work. Everything might have seemed chaotic and out of control, but Chad always kept a great attitude.

All of this creation work went on against the backdrop of the Winter Olympics that lay just ahead. Mitt Romney, former stake president of the Boston Massachusetts Stake, had helped rescue the struggling Salt Lake Olympic Committee as its chief executive officer and lifted the morale of the whole community with his tremendous ability and enthusiasm. No matter what had happened in the past, he confidently guided the immense project toward a successful winter extravaganza. We watched our friend from Belmont, Massachusetts, and his wife, Ann, take control of this project as if they had been made for it alone.

When it was necessary, we traveled to the countries where we were trying to perfect the program. On 4 November, for example, I returned to São Paulo to work with CES leaders. We were afforded much time during the annual CES convention in South America to promote the program and to train, teach, and interface with those who would carry the program directly to the young people in South America.

As earlier mentioned, the First Presidency added many other related assignments to our program, and no little complexity, by transferring a dozen or so other programs for us to integrate and figure out. For example, one program that a prominent Latter-day Saint family had established, provided loans for a particular segment of Church youth. CES had administered this, but PEF took on the day-to-day administration of it, integrating it within the PEF system. Happily, most programs transferred to us could be folded right into what we were doing. We continued to confront problems such as how to charge and collect interest, deal with inflation when it became extraordinary, and work with the details.

While all of this was going on, we were living in a jittery world and a nation that was not the same after the terrorist attacks of 11 September. War continued in Afghanistan and threatened in other places.

On 16 November, we handled about fifty loan applications. Our processes were tested again and proved to be feasible. While friends continued to send large donations, our major contributors were the hundreds of thousands of small donors in the wards and branches of the Church. Interest in the PEF remained high. I addressed the National Advisory Council of the Marriott Business School on Saturday, 17 November, discussing PEF.

We fought through the tough issues on how to administer a worldwide loan program, collect the loans, provide proper notices to borrowers, and achieve the right balance between being kind and helpful, yet businesslike in our procedures. We had legal problems to analyze and solve in dozens of countries. Fortunately, we had an excellent and practical attorney in Bill Atkin to guide us. And Church lawyers in key parts of the world knew the territories. They would often call on outstanding local attorneys to counsel with us.

The board of directors for the PEF continued to provide strong guidance and counsel. President Hinckley, as always, went right to the heart of matters with his questions. And through constant hard work the PEF team came up with answers to the questions that the board posed. Even though we weren't progressing as rapidly as I would have liked, we were solving problems every day, and the number of Church employees and friends who helped us steadily grew. The LDS Foundation, under the guidance of McLain Bybee, provided tremendous service, coordinating work with major and specialized donors. The Appropriations Committee of the Church helped us develop software to handle the complex loan and student application processes. The program was beginning to grow in numbers of applications and complexity of operation.

Ensign Peak Investments, the Church securities investment arm, invested the growing fund. Roger Clarke managed Ensign Peak. I visited with him about investment policy on 12 December 2001. He was exceptionally well qualified due to his extensive experience, educational background, and fine temperament. We felt comfortable having him handle the terribly important and difficult task of managing so large a fund.

The following illustrates the diversity of donations PEF has received. A holiday letter arrived at our offices from a family that included five children. It seems that the children had made an arrangement with their father to acquire snowmobiles for Christmas. The deal was that if they earned $1,000 each, the father would provide the balance of the cost for the five snow-mobiles. As the holidays approached, each of the children had earned the money they had agreed to raise. Following general con-ference in October 2001, during a family home evening, the father shared President Hinckley's report on PEF. The children, moved by what they heard and felt, all asked if they could donate their hard-earned $1,000 to PEF. The father agreed and added his promised amount to a wonderful donation to the fund.

At our loan committee meeting on 13 December, we received our first applications, three in number, from Brazil along with 349 additional applications from other places. We approved about 340 applications that day and expected 100 more the next week. The major areas sending in applications were Peru and Chile. The pro-gram was increasing in momentum as we had expected. We were ending the year with hundreds of loans granted and a program in place, all against the backdrop of terrorist attacks that had done major damage with thousands of lives lost during the year. War was raging in Afghanistan against the Taliban. Despite all of this and an economic recession that affected the world, the fund was growing at a tremendous and generous rate. The machinery to handle loans was beginning to function. A pivotal year—really an incredible year—closed. It had taken its toll on my health and energy but nothing from which I couldn't rebound. We all felt tremendous gratitude and optimism as we faced 2002.

CHAPTER SEVEN

"EDUCATION IS THE KEY
TO OPPORTUNITY"

*There is an old saying that if you give a man a
fish, he will have a meal for a day. But if you teach
him how to fish, he will eat for the remainder of his
life. . . . Education is the key to opportunity.*

PRESIDENT GORDON B. HINCKLEY, GENERAL CONFERENCE, 31 MARCH 2001

IN INTRODUCING THE PERPETUAL Education Fund to the
Church, President Hinckley affirmed that education is
the key to opportunity and economic advancement. But the
education he spoke of was vocational and technical—the kind
of education that can be put immediately to work in most communities. He was not so much interested in providing a liberal arts
education as a practical kind of training. The kind of instruction
he envisioned can raise a person and a community to a higher economic plane throughout the world, bringing hope and opportunity. But how could that kind of education become available to
those mired deep in poverty?

Perhaps another bit of history is relevant. Remember the millions of American men who either joined or were conscripted into
military service during World War II? These GIs, as we came to
know them, endured much and made real sacrifices in serving our

nation. In the process they gained maturity and became determined to fashion a bright future for themselves and enjoy a rich, full, post-war life.

A grateful nation enacted the Servicemen's Readjustment Act of 1944 for World War II veterans. This act included benefits on a scale never before known in history, including educational training at government expense, guaranteed loans for businesses, homes, and farms, as well as job counseling and placement. Those who served during the Korean War and the Vietnam War received similar benefits. During the life of the first GI Bill of Rights, as it was called, nearly 8 million World War II veterans received benefits. Some received vocational training, and nearly 2,200,000 World War II veterans attended universities and colleges. To that we could add about 1,200,000 Korean War veterans attending college under the benefit program.

In his bestselling book, *The Greatest Generation,* Tom Brokaw observed: "The GI Bill, providing veterans tuition and spending money for education, was a brilliant and enduring commitment to the nation's future. They (the GIs) were a new kind of army now, moving onto the landscapes of industry, science, art, public policy, all the fields of American life, bringing to them the same passions and discipline that had served them so well during the war. They helped convert a wartime economy into the most powerful peacetime economy in history.[1]

That tremendous example is further evidence of what can happen when eager young people are able to obtain an education. Ancient history provides similar reinforcement of this truth. As far back as AD 61–79, Pliny the Younger, considered one of the most learned men of his time in the Roman Empire, wrote in one of his famous letters: "When I was in my native town, the young son of a fellow townsman of mine came to greet me. I said to him, 'You are studying?' 'Yes,' 'Where?' 'At Medionlanum.' 'Why not here?' And his father—for he was together and had in fact brought the boy himself—[said], 'Because we have no teachers here.' 'Why [do you have] none? For it concerns you very much'—and, opportunely, numerous fathers were listening—'that your children for preference go to school here. For where would they either reside more pleasantly than in their native place or be kept more virtuous than under eyes of their parents, or at less expense than at home? How little [trouble], in that case, it is to collect money and hire teachers, and to add to their salaries what you now spend for lodgings, for travel arrangements [and], for those things which are purchased outside the town?'"[2]

Pliny seemed to know the answer to helping the disadvantaged back in that early day, and it was to educate young people in their own communities. President Hinckley got that right, too.

The second president of the United States, John Adams, had much to say about training and education. One of his most famous opinions was the following found in a letter written to his wife, Abigail from Paris, while he served as an envoy there. He wrote: "I must study politics and war that my sons may have liberty to study mathematics and philosophy. My sons ought to study mathematics and philosophy, geography, natural history, naval architecture, navigation, commerce, and agriculture in order to give their children a right to study paintings, poetry, music, architecture, statuary, tapestry, and porcelain."[3]

Adams joined others, including Thomas Jefferson, in the faith that education is key to building a great society. Jefferson had much to say on the subject, as well as personally showing the way by spending a great amount of time seeking practical knowledge about how to improve techniques of plowing and other agricultural practices and mechanics. University training, he felt, should provide both basic academic and practical knowledge. Award-winning historian and writer, Gordon S. Wood, in *The Radicalism of the American Revolution,* summarized early nineteenth century American concepts of education (including some of Jefferson's words) that helped build the most prosperous and successful economy in history:

"The new middle class extolled education, but not a classical or even a liberal arts education. They wanted education that was practical and useful, and why not? Had not the revolutionary leaders themselves told them that the people of the New World required a different kind of education from those of the Old World—'an useful American education,' said Jefferson, with everyone 'instructed in general, competently to the common business of life,' and genius employing its talents 'to the useful arts, to inventions for saving labor and increasing our comforts, to nourishing our health, to civil government, military science, & c.'"[4]

We should not forget to add the beliefs and example of that great early American, Benjamin Franklin, who spent a lifetime gaining knowledge, experimenting with electricity and other basic and practical scientific concepts, and in general learning all he could about the world around him. He believed that elected officials should not be paid and created a special revolving fund for Philadelphia and another for the city of his birth, Boston, by using the salary afforded him as president of the State of Pennsylvania to help educate the youth of promise in those cities. The money was to be loaned "to such young married artificers under the age of twenty-five years as have served in apprenticeship in the said town(s) and faithfully fulfilled the duties required in their indentures."[5] The loans were to be in small amounts, cosigned by two respectable citizens who vouched for the recipient's moral character, repaid in ten years, and thereafter loaned again. We can immediately see the similarities between Franklin's vision of what would benefit young adults and the principles of the PEF program.

One of my favorite characters in American history is Booker T. Washington, who shared his story in a book titled *Up from Slavery.* What made the difference in his life? How did he escape the menial labor that was predictable for a person of his race in the nineteenth century? He determined to attend a school called the Hampton Normal and Agricultural Institute in Virginia, 500 miles away from his home. Braving hardship and hunger, he made his way to the institute by walking and hitching rides in railroad cars. He arrived there, seeking admission, without having had either a bath or a change of clothes in days. The head teacher, seeing his determination to stay and attend the school but doubtful of his worth because of his appearance, asked him to sweep the recitation room. He did so over and over, dusting and cleaning the room four times. The "Yankee" woman inspected the floor and furniture, taking out her handkerchief and rubbing the woodwork, walls, table, and benches. Finally she quietly remarked, "I guess you will do to enter this institution."[6]

Most of us know something about the career that awaited Washington, but it all started with his education and training in the Hampton Normal and Agricultural Institute in Virginia. He spent his life providing both practical education relevant to jobs that communities needed and academic training using the books available in his day. He accomplished much. His theories concerning education coincide remarkably with the underlying values of the PEF. His bedrock belief was that practical education, combined with a work program conducted during and forming part of formal education, was the key to leading former slaves from their widespread poverty to achievement and acceptance in their communities. He was exhibit A to his thesis.

Many of our most public-spirited citizens, throughout history, provide evidence that President Hinckley was on target in declaring that providing opportunities for education, knowledge, and training are the best ways to help less-advantaged youths obtain jobs and escape lives of poverty and servitude. This is especially true if the education can be practical and locally obtained. It is even better if a way to promote self-reliance and self-respect is built into the program. As we have already seen, Franklin proved this could be done by establishing a loan fund to provide opportunities to deserving young adults. Let them have a chance, build in them self-reliance in place of a feeling of entitlement, and make it reasonable and possible to repay the loan, then let them go as far as their ability and ambition will take them. In effect, give young people a leg up and a push in the right direction. What they will accomplish will be a boon to themselves and to society.

President Hinckley seemed instinctively and inspirationally to know the way when he established PEF. He has embraced and is teaching the time-honored and proven principles that created in America a prosperous, middle-class society, whose members enjoy time beyond their employment for family, Church, and community building. Time will tell how far this work will take our own young people.

NOTES

1. Tom Brokaw, *The Greatest Generation* (New York: Random House, 1998), xx.
2. *Letters and Panegyricus of Pliny*, Betty Radice, trans. 2 vols. (London, Heinemann; Cambridge, Mass.: Harvard University Press, 1969), 279.
3. David G. McCullough, *John Adams* (New York: Simon & Schuster, 2001), 236–37.
4. Gordon S. Wood, *The Radicalism of the American Revolution* (New York: Vintage Books, 1993), 349.
5. H. W. Brands, *The First American: The Life and Times of Benjamin Franklin* (New York: Doubleday, 2000), 712–13.
6. Booker T. Washington, *Up From Slavery* (Grand Rapids, Mich.: Candace Press, 1996), 58.

NADINE, HAITI

In an area with 80 percent unemployment, Nadine is studying to become a teacher and she has already located employment. She will be a faithful leader where so many need so much.

CHAPTER EIGHT

PERFECTING AND EXPANDING

*Therefore, not leaving the principles of
the doctrine of Christ, let us go on
unto perfection.*

HEBREWS 6:1, JST

ONE OF THE UNKNOWNS IN establishing the PEF department
was whether Church members would provide the massive
voluntary support we would need to carry out a worldwide program of such magnitude. Another was whether the organization
of the Church could withstand the strain this vast new undertaking would place on it. Latter-day Saints all over the Church
answered the first question with a resounding YES! When the
reports of giving came in for December 2001, it was clear that
the size of the fund was already far ahead of what any of us had
anticipated. In the last month of 2001, the Saints and friends of
the Church had been tremendously generous. In monetary terms,
the future of the fund seemed assured. We soon realized, however,
that we would need much more money to meet the needs than
originally anticipated.

Giving away money is easy, but loaning it properly and

inducing repayment is difficult. With the fund seemingly assured of eventually securing sufficient financial means, the challenge for the PEF team was to create the gears, wheels, mechanisms, and structure that would find and make loans to those who were actually deserving and to ensure that the borrowers would repay those loans. To these ends we had worked in 2001, and we dedicated the year 2002 to perfect the processes.

We spent all morning on Friday, 4 January 2002, addressing the subject of the operations of the fund. Chad Evans led out in the effort. Coordination and infrastructure come at a cost in time, effort, and intelligent application of correct principles. Always we pled for divine guidance and tied our work to the words of our prophet and the scriptures. We expended much effort in expressing our gratitude to the generous people who helped, contributed, and offered service. Applications for loans started pouring in, and the loan committee and processing department had their hands full. What a great job Richard Cook, the Creers, and Debbie Muir were doing!

We continued to coordinate our work with the Presiding Bishopric: Bishop H. David Burton and his counselors Richard C. Edgley, and Keith B. McMullin, who provided hope and sound counsel. Their spiritual and business acumen were evident as we moved ahead, and they were tremendously helpful and cooperative.

Staff meetings were open and frank. With strong personalities aboard, we had to work at staying correlated, coordinated, and working with good feelings. One of the hardest hurdles to clear was the mechanism for collecting the loans. We tried several methods to achieve the desired result. We were still working in just five

Church areas: Mexico, Peru, Chile, Brazil, and the Philippines. (The latter had been approved, but training of our local teams lay ahead.) Eventually we worked out the legal, accounting, and relationship issues. Progress was slow but steady.

In our first board meeting of the New Year, held on Wednesday, 30 January, President Hinckley quietly declared without equivocation that we would have the resources we needed for the loan applications as they came. He also shared his insight into the future benefits of the fund, declaring that this would make a tremendous difference for the Church. He clearly saw the future of what we are doing. As always, he encouraged us to go forward with faith. I continued the practice, started in our first board meetings, of bringing new volunteers to the meeting so that the board would feel their spirit. President Hinckley was always gracious and full of encouragement to them.

On 31 January, David Clark and I left Salt Lake City for Guatemala. We had several purposes in mind for the trip. The principal reason for going to Central America was to learn more about their young returned missionaries and others of that age. We also wanted to begin the training of the constituencies that would give leadership to the program once we were cleared to commence it in their countries. At that time the Central America Area of the Church consisted of Guatemala, El Salvador, Honduras, Nicaragua, and Belize. All three members of the area presidency were local priesthood leaders. We needed time to get acquainted, train them, and hear from them what they considered to be the situation in each of these countries.

Our guide in Guatemala was Elder Israel Pérez of the area presidency and chairman of the area PEF committee. He has an extensive family business headquartered in his hometown of Quetzaltenango. His wife, Pilar, and he had 14 children, with 8 living. Almost the entire family works in the family business. They have the skills needed to make it work. We visited Fundet, the school the Clark Family Foundation had established, and saw young men and women hard at work training for occupations and employment. At the time of our trip, Guatemala had forty stakes, El Salvador sixteen, Honduras twenty, Nicaragua two, with none yet in Belize. The Church had four missions in Guatemala, two in El Salvador, three in Honduras, one in Nicaragua. The majority of the missionaries serving in those countries were homegrown. Of relevance to our program was that about 600–700 missionaries returned home each year to these countries. Many of these had little hope of getting training and good jobs. We hoped to improve that situation.

On Sunday, 4 February, we attended sacrament meeting on the temple grounds in Guatemala City. I couldn't remember such a fast and testimony meeting, featuring youngsters and teenagers who came to the stand in droves, awaiting their turn to express their testimonies and gratitude. The meeting could have gone on the entire day. We visited the temple where we met President Milton Smith, the youngest son of President Joseph Fielding Smith, and his wife. Then we visited the MTC where President and Sister Hopkins were busy training about 70 missionaries from various countries of Central America prior to their departure for missions in those countries. We felt a wonderful spirit there. In the afternoon we trained the leaders from all over Central America. I couldn't remember a more inspiring trip in my lifetime.

All of these countries we visited had impressive leaders and carried on an outstanding Church program.

While the world concentrated on the Winter Olympics in Salt Lake City, we concentrated on taking the PEF program to the world. On Monday, 11 February, I flew with Rex Allen to Manila, Philippines, to inaugurate the PEF there. I stayed with Elder Merrill C. Oaks, the area president. Tim Sloan, who worked with the department that administers the Church employment program, traveled with us. Elder Oaks had delegated to his counselor, Elder John M. Madsen, the assignment to chair the area PEF committee. Elder Madsen had done an outstanding job preparing for the coming of PEF. We began training with that committee on Wednesday, 13 February. The area presidency was most supportive and generous. Elder Ángel Abrea, an old colleague and friend, was the other member of the presidency.

While in Manila, we trained a representative group of young adults, testing our procedures and teaching leaders how to apply the program. We held a well-attended fireside one evening for an enthusiastic group of young adults and their leaders. Outstanding music was provided by two choirs, and a great spirit along with an outpouring of love filled the chapel.

On my trip home from Manila, I read the brief account of how missionary work was initiated in the Philippines by Elder Gordon B. Hinckley, then of the Twelve. President Joseph Fielding Smith had dedicated the land for the preaching of the gospel on 21 August 1955, and President Hinckley commenced the work on 28 April 1961. The story is an inspiring one, especially when we see the tremendous number of members and stakes now in those islands.

February proved to be yet another pivotal month in the establishment of this program, with our various efforts to open doors and establish the framework in Central America and the Philippines. We were on our way. Our board meeting on 27 February was, as always, most helpful. We gave the board a full report on our progress and our many challenges, and we in turn received great support. February was also a month of outstanding success for Salt Lake City and Utah because of the nearly flawless handling of the Winter Olympics. Many thought they were the finest in Olympic history. The state and even the Church garnered favorable worldwide notice.

On the first day of March, the PEF loan committee required four hours to handle all of the pending loan applications. It all took time and effort, and not everything went smoothly. Solving the many issues and making decisions required much time and discussion. The work of PEF has gone forward, but not always without ripples. Still, we found that if we kept our hearts and minds open to ideas and feelings, in time the Spirit would guide us onto the right path. We felt confidence in the ultimate success of the venture.

Business leaders consistently kept in touch with what we were doing and pledged conceptual and financial support to the fund. On Tuesday, 12 March, Chad left for Peru to solve problems and continue training. Brother Gordon Creer joined him two days later, after his visa for Brazil came following a delay. On Tuesday, 12 March, I went back over all of our policy materials. I was impressed that in most respects it had withstood the test of the nine months that had ensued since we drafted them and the board had approved the approach we had devised.

In 2002, with First Presidency approval, we formed a corporation called the Perpetual Education Fund, Inc. The PEF team believed that a nonprofit corporation would prove useful and beneficial to a program that had to enter into contractual business arrangements. The existence of a corporation would also be valuable, since some donors preferred donating money to such an entity rather than to the Church as a whole. Boyd Black of the Office of General Counsel handled the formation work and did a splendid job. On 20 March, we held our first board meeting for the new corporation to elect officers and enact organizational resolutions. With the approval of our PEF board of directors, I was elected chairman of the board, president, and CEO. Rex J. Allen, Chad L. Evans, and Richard E. Cook were elected vice presidents. The corporation is wholly owned by the Church and has the IRS Section 503 exemption for donations as a result of that.

On Tuesday, 26 March, I met with Paul V. Johnson who heads the program of Church schools, institutes of religion, and seminaries. While on his recent trip through Latin America, Paul discovered some concerns held by institute workers regarding their roles in administering PEF. The additional workload was extensive and worrisome. We knew it would be. Our solution to their concerns was to ask them to add volunteers to their staff to work on the application and processes necessary to make the program real and ensure its success in collections. As we earlier observed, it is easy to give away money, but establishing a program with gears and wheels to provide recipients with monthly statements, compute interest, and work with the borrowers takes much more effort. In addition, starting a new program always takes more time than continuing one that is in motion.

Creating the PEF program from scratch has been akin to setting in motion a massive wheel weighing several tons. It requires tremendous pressure to start the wheel turning from a standstill position. But eventually, when everything is moving in unison and procedures have been refined, it practically runs itself. We had been managing a startup, and it had been challenging for our CES partners as well as us. All involved, however, have had the attitude that PEF will go forward and that it will be successful. Nevertheless, people do suffer when they are loaded with work beyond their capacity, and PEF does add to the workload of many of our colleagues. In particular, after applications are approved; papers still need signing, students require ongoing assistance and support, and local Church leaders must deal with the unexpected personal trials that arise in the lives of some loan recipients, trials that impact their ability to meet the promised performance.

The next day, 27 March, we told the board about the added workload that PEF had placed on local leaders. Brother Paul V. Johnson of CES stated that no one in CES had complained to him and that all believed in the inspired nature and great potential of PEF. During the meeting we described for the board the software program that had been developed to assist students and leaders to understand the program, apply for loans on line, and assist in the managing of the complex processes involved. The Web site that is a part of the new program contained the application. In any place in the world where a computer and Internet were available, those involved could access the Web site. We also explained that students would need access to computers at institutes of religion participating in the program. The board gave approval in concept to obtaining and installing the needed computers for the use of students. Board members expressed joy in the progress of PEF. The report of the concern on workload increase in the field, they felt, was evidence that institute directors are required to be directly involved in helping young people prepare for their careers and their lives.

The transitioning of some of the preexisting programs that were transferred to us had taken time and effort. We continued to work on that process during March and made progress with several of the loan programs that we were assisting CES to administer. We renamed the IEF program the PEF-B program. PEF-A was reserved for the basic PEF program of occupational and technical training as distinguished from university and professional training covered by PEF-B. On that note we ended March.

During the ensuing general conference, we intruded onto the busy schedules of overseas area presidencies who were in Salt Lake City to train them in the principles and procedures of PEF. At the Saturday morning session of general conference, President Hinckley reported to the Church on the progress of the PEF. Among other things he shared: "The contributions of generous Latter-day Saints have come in to assure us that this endeavor is now on a solid foundation." He added: "We will need more yet, but already it has been demonstrated that vast good will come of this undertaking. Young men and women in the underprivileged areas of the world, young men and women who for the most part are returned missionaries, will be enabled to get good educations that will lift them out of the slough of poverty in which their forebears for generations have struggled. They will marry and go forward with skills that will qualify them to earn well and take their places in society where they can make a substantial contribution.

They will likewise grow in the Church, filling positions of responsibility and rearing families who will continue in the faith."[1]

He cited one testimonial from a PEF recipient and concluded
with: "And so it goes, my brothers and sisters. As this great work
moves across the earth, we are blessing now some 2,400 young
people. Others will be blessed."[2]

We all felt the passion and enthusiasm of President Hinckley,
and it motivated Church members to continue their growing partnership with this outreach program. Those of us directly involved
in its leadership felt the strength of President Hinckley's support
and participation. We were motivated to redouble our efforts.

On Monday, 8 April, after the general sessions were over, we
had lunch with CES leaders from around the world who were
meeting in convention. We also met with the zone administrators
who lead the program around the world and discussed our
progress and concerns. These good men and women shared our
vision and enthusiasm for the work. We showed them the 14-
minute video and responded to a few questions. After general
conference, we decided to add another missionary couple to give
leadership to the programs we were administering. The couple we
chose, Ronald Ririe and his wife, Afton, were a wonderful addition to our team. Ronald had served in the West Central States
Mission with me many decades before. His career had been with
IBM, and Sister Ririe was equally qualified and willing to help.

During general conference, a team from one of the largest
vocational training institutions in Mexico came to visit Church
headquarters and get better acquainted with us. We met with
them on 10 April. They enjoyed getting a feeling, not only for

PEF, but also for the Church as an institution. Chad looked after them for us.

We continued an active program of outreach, responding to many invitations to teach and speak. We also confronted the issue of sending out PEF missionaries to serve in areas particularly impacted with extra work because of PEF. We had to resolve differing opinions on how to accomplish all of this, and we made progress by discussing various approaches in a meeting held on 16 April, during which most of our concerns were resolved. On 23 April, Richard Cook left for Brazil to work on financial matters there, Chad Evans prepared to go to Peru for training, and Rex Allen continued his many projects. In our April board meeting, we planned to demonstrate our Web site and show how it worked. The Church technology system chose our meeting time as the moment to crash, but Rex was able to talk the board through the process. Our work was becoming more routine as we solved problems one by one.

As mentioned above, the Church had transferred Brent Plowman from the Finance Department to PEF to act as its controller. We introduced the Riries and Brent to our staff at the loan committee meeting on 9 May. Work continued with staff meetings, loan committee meetings, board meetings, conferences, and speaking engagements. We prepared to send a couple, Elder D. Duke and Sister Alice N. Cowley to Brazil to help with the program and particularly to find many who needed help in obtaining training and jobs but didn't know where and how to obtain it. Getting the right visas would take time. We planned for Brother Wilford A. and Sister Phyllis R. Cardon to follow the Cowleys in their Brazilian service. Both the Cardons and Cowleys had served as mission presidents and companions in Brazil many years prior. During the years following thier missions, working as individuals, they had done an immense amount of good helping their missionaries better themselves and were enthusiastic about PEF. One of the ways our fund was growing was that some members terminated their own private foundations and contributed the assets to PEF, being convinced that this work was more helpful than what they had been doing. Help came also from Church members who had lost their spouses in death and who suggested in their obituaries that instead of flowers, donations be made to PEF. We were amazed at the ingenuity and generosity of the Saints, old and young, who believed in this program.

On 12 June 2002, President Hinckley addressed the World Affairs Council in Los Angeles for the third time. He asked the PEF team for more specific information on the progress of PEF and featured the program as part of his remarks in Los Angeles. Truly the program was reaching out to many, in and out of the Church. All who learned about it and what we were doing resonated with its concepts. Applications kept pouring in. In our loan committee meeting held on Friday, 14 June, we had 230 applications to consider.

At the PEF board meeting on 19 June, the board granted approval to a renewed effort to let Church members and others know about PEF. The board also approved extending the program to all of the remaining countries of Latin America. We now needed to train leaders in South America North, South America South, Central America, and possibly the Caribbean areas. The board also approved the calls of Presidents Cowley and Cardon and their wives to represent us in Brazil. We now approached the

July break, noting in staff meetings that though the work was increasing, the program was up and working. Some matters had become routine, and efficient systems had been developed to speed the work along. We felt less and less like a startup and more and more like an established program with a global reach that had limitless potential for blessing the lives of young members of the Church and their families.

That summer we benefited by having Elizabeth Watkins Gerner work with us as an intern. She was a graduate student studying philanthropic programs and nonprofit organizations. She also managed her family foundation. With his experience in training and academic research, Rex Allen gave Elizabeth some useful assignments, helping us assess what we were doing and why we were doing it.

Richard Cook led out in training international controllers during the second week of July and Chad Evans held a committee meeting with the Implementation Committee. That committee comprised the people in all the departments with heavy responsibility for PEF—those involved in the actual work of operating the program. The Implementation Committee, chaired by Chad, together with the Finance Committee, chaired by Richard, kept the inner workings of PEF straight and acted as hands-on problem-solving committees. Sometimes their duties overlapped, but both played huge roles in our work.

On Monday, 8 July, I worked out a draft of a strategic plan for PEF. I worked on such questions as precisely who we were trying to serve with PEF, in what countries we should operate, what types of education we should encourage in the future, what size the fund needed to become to accomplish our goals, and what organization PEF would need in order to handle the program five or ten years out. With the number of loans and complexity of the organization, we would need qualified help in the department for the foreseeable future. We felt much of that help could come from retired couples, such as the Riries and Creers.

On Wednesday, 17 July, I had lunch with a business organization that meets in Salt Lake City from time to time to discuss estate planning interests and concerns. They are top-flight men and women in estate planning and related legal fields. I spoke to them at their request about PEF. The implications of their interest are that men and women are thinking strongly of bequeathing charitable gifts to PEF as a part of their estate plans. The LDS Foundation works closely with this group. Other similar groups have been organized in other cities.

We thought the flow of applications would slow during the summer, but it didn't.

On Monday, 5 August, the Church's legal staff from all over the world held a series of meetings to discuss problems. Their assignment for PEF was to help us overcome legal obstacles in each country where PEF would eventually operate. Their goal for PEF, in consultation with excellent local attorneys, was to keep us from legal problems in countries where PEF was making loans. They were, therefore, very interested in an update on the program. They had already been of immense assistance to us in the countries of Peru, Chile, Mexico, Brazil, and the Philippines where we were up and running. And dozens of other countries were on our radar screens.

On 12–13 August, we held all-day training meetings with three couples who had been called to represent us and assist in the work in Brazil and the Philippines. Rex Allen, our chief trainer, was beautifully prepared and did some of the finest training any of us had witnessed. I then went to Los Angeles to meet with the Brazilian Consul General. We needed to know what kind of visa the Cowleys and Cardons would need to spend six months or more in the country representing PEF. He wanted to know all about the program. At the conclusion of our conference, he asked our advice on several matters of concern to him in his work and expressed his admiration for PEF. The kind of visa we needed would take several levels of approval, but it was the safe way to proceed. He promised help and subsequently gave it. The first visas came through for the Cowleys in November.

On 15 August, I met with Boyd Black of the Office of General Counsel for the Church. He was in charge of creating the PEF Corporation, and has continued helping us draft some of our legal documents. We have found our Church attorneys able, practical, and helpful in sharing and solving problems.

On a Friday evening, Shirley and I went to Provo to speak to the Academy of LDS Dentists, an association of dentists from all over the United States. The large banquet room in the downtown Provo Marriott was full of men and women who showed great interest in the work.

As I prepared to pass out agenda notebooks for the August meeting of the PEF board of directors, I discovered that the First Presidency had made changes on the board. Elder M. Russell Ballard had been released from the board to spend his full energy as Chairman of the Missionary Executive Council. Elder Richard G. Scott had taken Elder Ballard's place as chairman of the Executive Committee for BYU and other Church schools, and as such would serve on the board. Elder Robert D. Hales was also added to the board. Already, in little over a year, there had been four changes on the board. On 27 August, the day before the board meeting, Richard Cook and I made a presentation before the Church Budget Committee, chaired by President Hinckley. We gave the committee a good review of our progress to date and shared what we expected to do for the next year. We also outlined concerns and problems for them to know and think about. This was a high level meeting that included the top financial officers of the Church. We followed this with the board meeting on 28 August.

During September our key staff members traveled to a number of places to solve problems, continue training, and inaugurate the program in the rest of Latin America. It was an immense undertaking. Richard Cook and Chad Evans completed training in the remainder of South America. Rex Allen and I trained all of the key people of Central America, gathered in beautiful Guatemala City on 16 September. Bill Atkin of the Office of General Council was there and helped us evaluate the legal situation in Guatemala, El Salvador, Honduras, and Nicaragua. The quality of our leaders, both temporal and spiritual, was wonderful in Central America.

As part of the training, we focused attention on the step-by-step financial procedures. Richard and Chad, with the able assistance of Elder Creer, had worked hard to iron out the bugs in our systems. The Director of Temporal Affairs for the area was a former mission president and stake president, with excellent skills, deep spirituality, and a positive attitude. The controller was an experienced North American, with a rich financial background.

We enjoyed having Greg Clark, the legal advisor for the area, and Bill Atkin with us in most of our meetings.

Following our training in Guatemala City, on Wednesday, 18 September, we flew to Santo Domingo in the Dominican Republic, where all the future Caribbean participants in this program gathered for a seminar under their area president, Elder Gene R. Cook. Elder Cook stayed with us for our training meetings and participated. While there we met with the missionaries and director of the MTC, as we had done in Guatemala City. Assembled in the training meetings were all the leaders we needed from the Dominican Republic, Haiti, Puerto Rico, Jamaica, and the West Indies. Since I had once been area president for the Caribbean, it was a thrilling homecoming for me. We also met in a fireside with the young adults of Santo Domingo. The turnout was excellent and the spirit high. With the simultaneous training going on with Chad and Richard in South America, we had now covered all of Latin America. We found enthusiasm and cooperation every place we went. We came back to Salt Lake City with our spirits buoyed and uplifted.

Our next trip would be to Africa. We sensed the growing influence of PEF. Problems were also multiplying, but we would meet some of them directly at the October 2002 semiannual general conference. We had sent invitations to the area presidencies to meet with us on a voluntary basis during their brief stay at Church headquarters. Virtually every overseas area presidency accepted our invitation. We met with them in four different meetings. Many honest and tough questions came up, but we found everyone cooperative and the sharing and training sessions useful. At the general priesthood meeting on Saturday evening,

5 October, President Hinckley gave a stewardship report on several subjects to the brethren. One of these was PEF. By then we had about 5,000 loans outstanding, and the number was growing daily. His reports have had a wonderful effect on the desire of the Saints to donate regularly to the fund, and they were doing it. It seemed that in every social gathering we attended, I was called on to report on PEF. The interest seemed universal and remained high through the year and a half that had elapsed since President Hinckley announced the formation of PEF.

On Tuesday, 15 October, Chad and I departed for Johannesburg, South Africa, where we had a wonderful experience introducing the leaders to PEF and preparing them for the time the full program could be inaugurated there. Elder Steven Snow chaired our meetings as chairman of the area PEF committee. The area CES director was an old friend, Jim Ritchie, with his wife, Carolyn, as assistant. We knew we had to get it right at the beginning to be successful. Chad carried the training load with spirit and skill. He had been invaluable in the formulation of this work. The challenges faced by that region are unique, but we left confident that there could be, in the not-too-distant future, a large, successful PEF program in Africa. While we were in Africa, Rex Allen was in Asia, starting with the Philippines and then working his way through Hong Kong and into the Australia and Pacific area, anticipating the coming of the program in those parts. He traveled alone this time and brought us valuable information about the needs and concerns there.

On Tuesday, 22 October, we met with the owner and key employee of the Mortgage Computer Company that provided the software for our loans. We talked things over and found the owner knowledgeable and cooperative. We needed them to transition to a Web-based program and they explained their plans to make that transition in the next year or so. There is no end to the complexities of starting a program as far-reaching as this one. Richard Cook and I made a more in-depth presentation than we usually did to the board on Wednesday, 30 October. We felt their full support and especially enjoyed the kind words of the board chairman about the progress we had made. Although much remained to be done, we felt that the program was now established and working. We felt we could proceed to finish the work on the foundation we had laid.

Notes

1. Gordon B. Hinckley, in Conference Report, April 2002, 5.
2. Ibid.

Vanderlei and Rosalia, Brazil

Vanderlei Lira returned from his successful mission to very difficult conditions. His lack of education forced him to common labor and the Lira family sometimes suffered from lack of food and decent housing.

The PEF was introduced and Vanderlei received a loan and entered school. After his graduation, the school offered him a job as Safety Manager over construction of a large new campus. Vanderlei serves on the high council and his stake president describes him as a great father and leader, "a giant who has been liberated by opportunity."

CHAPTER NINE

HOW AND WHY IT WORKS

*And there are diversities of operations, but it is
the same God which worketh all in all.*

1 CORINTHIANS 12:6

THE PEF PROGRAM HELPS less-advantaged young people rise
above poverty and join those who enjoy the privilege of
working and earning a decent living. The foregoing chapters have
described the process of creating the necessary organization and
have placed PEF in its historical context. We now take a closer
look at why education and training are the answers and how we
have tried to strike the right balance in opening opportunities for
recipients.

I earlier referred to my years spent in working with young
missionaries for The Church of Jesus Christ of Latter-day Saints. I
consider that work and those years as the most important work of
my life, excepting family life. Some missionaries came from families that provided them with vision, concepts, and opportunities
to compete successfully in the world of work. Many young men
and women, however, had never discussed their futures with an

adult, not even with their parents. As is true with others involved in the same work, as a mission president, I always encouraged my missionaries, as they completed their terms of service, to look to the future. We discussed together the importance of education and preparing for life and a lifetime of service. These were young people who had voluntarily worked day after day and night after night in the difficult business of inviting people to change their lives by embracing the gospel of Jesus Christ. Their work involved contacting people in their homes, on the streets, and on buses and streetcars, and it involved teaching them principles and gospel doctrines. It was hard work and most of them grew tremendously as individuals as a result of their service.

As they concluded that service and prepared to return to their homes, some were ready to tackle anything and everything. You could not hold them back. But what were they to do as an encore? How were they to find their way in the world of work? For those who had grown up in circumstances that gave them a chance to succeed, their return meant that ahead were opportunities and privileges. All they needed to do was to roll up their sleeves and go to work. For them, answers to the question of what was next were natural and easy. Just let them loose and they would find their way. But others went home to grinding poverty and hopelessness. In spite of what they had learned about hard work and devotion during their missions, they were in danger of sinking not only into deprivation but into despair.

The following true narrative is typical of my and others' experience in the mission field. The particular young man of this story had come to his mission in Idaho from a fine home, but had never discussed his future with parents or other adults in any depth. His prior interests were girls, hanging out at the beach, and cars. He had given no thought to finding a way to make a living for his future wife and family. His grades were average or less in high school. At least he had a formal education, although he took minimal advantage of it. During his mission, having enjoyed the example of hardworking parents, he proved a diligent missionary who was successful in a variety of assignments. He had found himself more able than he thought, as many missionaries do. We had great confidence that if he continued in the pattern established on his mission he would be a faithful member of the Church, be successful and useful in society, and would find a fine person to marry. We also believed that he would be a great father, but we worried about the lack of direction and planning for his life.

When I asked him about his plans, he said he had none, but enjoyed working outdoors doing gardening and manual labor. I supported his love of working with his hands, doing tasks he enjoyed but suggested that even if he made his living doing manual labor he would find himself in the world of business and therefore needed to get into school to learn more about things like management, accounting, and planning. I suggested that with his background and mission experience he might enjoy majoring in accounting, economics, or business administration. I urged him to at least get a degree in something like that in addition to finding a way to follow his natural interests. I also suggested that after he had worked for awhile, he might consider seeking an MBA. We did what we could to raise his vision to a higher level to help him see his possibilities, all in an interview lasting an hour. Always positive, he thanked me and soon left us for home where he was reunited with his great family.

During the next four years I heard nothing from him. One day, out of the blue, a letter arrived from him. He first shared his gratitude for all he had learned during his mission. Then he said he had always tried to follow my counsel and had done so after he arrived home. He found work in the field he enjoyed and with money he saved from his employment and the help of his parents he also enrolled in a university. Four years later he was graduating with a degree in accounting, having attained a 3.6 grade point average. A number of employment offers had resulted due to his training. He had followed his interest in working with his hands by starting a part-time gardening business as a side venture, but made his primary living in the field of accounting. We heard from him again from time to time, mostly through his wife. His company had advanced him to a position of one of its top financial officers. His family was growing, and he was serving as elders quorum president in his ward. He and his wife had achieved a solid place in the community.

What would the results be if we could open opportunities like those for thousands of less-advantaged young men and women all over the world? What if we could provide financial aid to pay for tuition, books, supplies, and fees by way of a loan to be repaid after training? That, indeed, was the vision President Hinckley shared with me the night he called me in Frankfurt, Germany. When he announced the program in general priesthood meeting on 31 March 2001, President Hinckley merely hinted at the inspired source of the program he described. His initial announcement was so complete with details, principles, and doctrines that it struck virtually the whole Church as inspired. Almost everyone who heard his initial announcement of PEF, instantly gained an testimony that it was not only inspired, but also was right for the times and the needs of young people.

In essence, PEF was as a call to a second mission for returned missionaries and others of that age, especially those who were without opportunities. They had left behind their youth and all that was important to them and now needed to find their way into the larger world of education and work. We needed to let them know how serious and important that new phase of their lives was and give them a little boost.

While I was in Brazil not long ago, an outstanding brother translated for me while I trained Church leaders in the principles of PEF. I asked him after one session what he did for a living. He answered that he was the president of a major North American company in Brazil. I then asked him how he had achieved this great place among his people. He answered that it all stemmed from his bishop arranging for him to receive several years of English training during his teenage years, and providing financial assistance as well. Later a group of businessmen had given him a loan that enabled him to obtain a master's degree in business. He had repaid the loan and advanced to his present position by hard work. Along the way he had served as a stake president and mission president, but it all originated with the opportunities that his Church leaders had opened up for him in his youth.

Many of our young people have lacked the training and financial help to get beyond their poverty and gain skills sufficient to qualify them for available good jobs. One of the first loans granted after we commenced with the PEF program was to a young woman in Mexico. She wanted to become a dental hygienist and that, she told us, would allow her to earn some $400 per month instead of the approximately $100 she was then earning. We granted her a modest loan that enabled her to start her training. During that first year of training she raised her income by fifty percent with the offer of a new job in a dental office. During her last year of training, she learned that she would earn more than $600 per month when she completed her schooling.

In his initial announcement of PEF, President Hinckley explained this principle by saying: "I believe the Lord does not wish to see His people condemned to live in poverty. I believe He would have the faithful enjoy the good things of the earth." As the well-known scripture avers, "there is enough and to spare" (D&C 104:17). But the Lord also states in that same section that help for the poor "must needs be done in [His] own way" (v.16). This implies that initiatives to help the less-advantaged should promote resourcefulness, self-reliance, dignity, and self-respect. Throwing money at a problem has usually proved unhelpful and even harmful. Helping people help themselves builds people and allows them to maintain their self-respect and independence. Independence and dignity and a feeling of providing for oneself is vitally important and is the Lord's way to assist the poor.

These are the principles we have built into PEF. Some have suggested that the young people for whom the initiative has been designed should be given grants or scholarships instead of expecting them to repay loans. In most cases this undermines the principles on which PEF is based. By doing it the way designed in the program, the recipients of loans not only help themselves, but by repaying their loans they help those that come after them. And showing Church members the great need for PEF, and asking them to contribute by way of voluntary donations, builds and strengthens those who respond.

Creating PEF in this way has also effectively captured something deep within the people, as evidenced by the hundreds of thousands who have gladly and voluntarily invested in the fund, with regular and heartfelt donations. The Saints have always had feelings of love and charity for the less-advantaged, but this program has provided the avenue to express these sentiments in a powerful, beneficial, and practical way. The vast international scope of the initiative immediately caught the imagination of the people, and tying it historically to past initiatives to assist the poor, such as the Perpetual Emigrating Fund, has given it a tie with history that has proved a remarkable motivation to many of us.

Deep inside the Saints has always resided a desire to help. With the PEF the prophet has shown them what is needed to lift the youth and how to help in that effort. As President Hinckley said, quoting President Joseph F. Smith, "A religion which will not help a man in this life will not likely do much for him in the life to come." The Saints all over the world have resonated to President Hinckley's call to take seriously our responsibility to help young adult members "become self-reliant and successful." He asked us to take up this matter as "a very serious obligation."

It doesn't take too much imagination to see the future benefits of the modern PEF. It surely will build tens of thousands of young people by providing practical training and education otherwise unavailable to them. Those despairing of their ability to support a family will, through PEF, gain new hope. As they receive training directly relevant to the work that needs to be done in their countries, they will have opportunities to join the workforce and contribute to the economic strength of their countries. A community is no stronger than the technical abilities of its work force. As our young members complete their training, obtain good employment, and enjoy better incomes as a result, they will be able to repay their loans and help those coming behind them who need the same kind of help. They will also have the satisfaction of knowing that they have helped themselves and, as President Hinckley explained, "They will enjoy a wonderful sense of freedom because they have improved their lives, not though a grant or gift, but through borrowing and then repaying. They can hold their heads high in a spirit of independence."

A side benefit of this initiative to the Church is that these young people will join the rolls of tithe-payers, allowing the Church to continue to build chapels and temples, develop stronger communities, and provide leadership in every part of the world. Thus, President Hinckley predicted, "The Church will be much stronger for their presence in the areas where they live." He prophesied that "God will prosper this effort and it will bring blessings, rich and wonderful, upon the heads of thousands."

To motivate those needing a loan we have built into the program a small rate of interest that begins shortly after they have completed their training. Missionaries have been called to help provide loan servicing. The fund grows through contributions and through repayment by loan recipients. Thus, as the need increases, the fund will increase.

The administration of this vast program is in the hands of area presidencies, CES area directors, local institute directors, directors of temporal affairs, area controllers, employment directors, stake presidents, bishops, and other leaders already in place. In other words, as President Harold B. Lee discovered in instituting the Church Welfare Program in the 1930s, all we needed to do was harness the energy of the priesthood of God to accomplish the work that needed to be done. This is not to say that thousands of hours of work and effort are not needed from these officers throughout the Church, but the organization everywhere was already in place to get this work accomplished.

While loan recipients would be ambitious young men and women with a desire and need for education, training, and gainful employment, they would not all be returned missionaries. In the first year of this initiative, about 60% of the recipients were men and 40% women. Of the men, about 85% have been returned missionaries and about 30% of the women have also filled missions.

As Pliny the Younger observed, there is great value in having the young people trained close to home in schools available there. They are more likely to build and strengthen their communities and the Church if they gain their educations at home. This principle also allows many of them to live at home while pursuing their goals, an important consideration, since loans given to recipients do not include funds for room and board. The recipients are also encouraged by the policies of the program to attend institutes of religion where they can continue their study of the scriptures and Church history, strengthening their testimonies and faithfulness.

The kind of schooling recommended depends on the jobs that are available in their communities. As a condition to receiving a loan, the young adult must take a brief course in career training and development that enables them to see what employment opportunities are available in their communities and assess their apptitudes, interests, and abilities. Thus the training, like that provided by community colleges and vocational institutions in the United States, is more relevant to the needs of the communities than is a general and classical education, as desirable as that may be.

A look at a batch of recent applications for loans from a South American country revealed the following occupational goals: automobile mechanic, banking clerk, clothing maker, computer network systems engineer, computer maintenance worker, computer programmer, electronic technician, environmental technician, hair stylist, hotel administrator, marketing and sales specialist, Microsoft certified systems engineer, natural gas technician, nurse, nutritionist, pathology lab technician, language translator, radiology technician, secretary, telecom technician, and Web technician. Note the practical and technical nature of these educational goals.

One 27-year-old returned missionary from Brazil, studying to become a radiology technician, reported: "I came home from my mission six years ago and eventually found a wonderful wife. However, all my efforts to gain an education were frustrated. The free courses I took were ineffective, and the good courses were expensive and, therefore, totally inaccessible to us. When the Perpetual Education Fund was announced, it gave me new hope about becoming self-reliant, about having a promising career. Today I am training to become a radiology technician thanks to a loan from the Perpetual Education Fund. After my graduation I will find a job that will give me the time and money to take care of my family, help me serve better in the Church, and eventually enable me to attend college."

A loan recipient from Colombia wrote: "The Perpetual Education Fund was an answer to my companions' faith, and the prayers of many others. Now I am achieving that dream (to go to school, work, and get married). I am attending one of the best schools in my city. My desires and motivation are higher than ever. I can see how I will be able to help my family, the Church, and others, and I will return in many ways the assistance given me. I am so grateful once again to see the fulfillment of the Lord's promise to 'always protect his sheep.'"

Such testimonials already number in the thousands. In the years to come, we shall see the tremendous change that this program will bring to the lives of individuals and families. It will provide leaders for the Church and build the economies and strength of the communities where these young people reside. PEF is a blessing also to the hundreds of thousands of men, women, and children who have contributed to the fund and who enjoy the satisfaction of having rendered justice and mercy to their fellow-citizens in the kingdom of God. The creation of PEF has bestowed on prosperous Church members a glorious opportunity to help young people around the world. Others have been out doing related projects in a wonderful way, doing much good. This is a chance for all of us to be part of an inspired initiative that is vast and grand in scale.

One last observation is that PEF may point the way for other organizations, including governments, to raise the level of their communities and countries by establishing comparable programs. One ambassador from a South American country, after we had explained what we were doing in his country, immediately said: "We need to learn from what you are doing and adopt similar principles and programs in my country." Not all programs designed to help the less-advantaged have helped. We can't be sure that an initiative like PEF would work outside a loving, family-oriented Church, but there are good people in all countries and organizations around the world who are doing tremendous things. Some of them may adopt and adapt PEF, at least its principles. In PEF we have seen some of the answers to the question of how to raise people out of poverty and give them opportunity and hope.

In the next chapter we summarize additional actual experiences of PEF participants as the third year drew to its close.

CHAPTER TEN

REALIZING THE DREAM

Beware of rashness, but with energy and sleepless
vigilance go forward and give us victories.
ABRAHAM LINCOLN IN A LETTER DATED 26 JANUARY 1863

EXPECTATIONS FOR PEF WERE sky high. The prophet had been unequivocal in his promises and declarations, and we were now well into our third year. The questions were changing. People wanted to know if the program was meeting expectations? Were the loan recipients paying back their loans? Have some of them graduated, and if so were they getting good jobs? In short, the questions being asked could be summarized as: Are we having success as President Hinckley envisioned? How had we done in making a prophet's vision become a practical reality? Have the youth grasped the opportunity and shown that they could do it?

We decided to send a team to search out the answers to these questions by meeting the young men and women who had been assisted by the fund and who had graduated or were well along in their goals. We wanted to capture on film what they were thinking and saying, and we wanted to meet them in person and see their faces.

We knew that not all recipients would have total success in meeting their goals. We were experienced and practical enough to know that with as many loans as we had granted, some recipients would have stumbled and fallen along the way. Achievement is never in a straight upward line. The program was wonderfully and spiritually conceived, but now the time for planning and dreaming had given way to real life. We knew we were dealing with young people who often had little background in borrowing, attending school, making and reaching goals, and budgeting their money and other resources. We had tried to meet the needs of all comers in the approved countries, provided they met the worthiness and other standards in their applications. We were not selecting the cream of the crop. Unless applicants demonstrated real needs and well-conceived goals, we had no loans to offer.

In evaluating the applications we received, the loan committee insisted that the applicants have plans that made good sense after taking our career training course called "Planning for Success." And most of them had taken career training with the Church Employment Resource Centers in addition. Our expectations were realistic, but high. And we were not disappointed in what we found.

Our team of professionals, under Rex Allen's personal supervision, talked to hundreds of PEF young adults in most of the countries where the program had been introduced and was operating. In those first years we had granted loans to over 10,000 young adults. Our projections were that in the next six or seven years we would have made some 65,000 loans. It was vital that we keep close to those loan recipients and keep the program moving in the right direction. Our team interviewed some just beginning the program, some in the middle of their education, and many who had completed their training and were embarked in various careers. We include some of their faces with this chapter and share some typical stories illustrating our findings and the very real impact of PEF in the lives of these young people.

From Guatemala you will see a marvelous group of students, all receiving training in a school named Fundet, established by the David Clark Family Foundation with an emphasis on vocational training, internships, and preparation for good employment in such vocations as electricity, automobile mechanics, cosmetology, and refrigeration. Refrigeration seems to be training that is much in demand in many countries. These are outstanding young people.

Also included is a picture of about 300 PEF trainees in various schools located in Peru. You can sense by looking at these students the kind of young people they are and the great potential for leadership they possess. Another picture is of a group from the Philippines making pillows for sale as a means of making their PEF payments while they are in school.

Now for some of their stories in their own words or, in some of the stories, as we have summarized their words from notes we took during visits with them.

One of the students in Rio de Janeiro said: "PEF has opened new horizons for me. It has expanded my vision. PEF has given my wife and me a great opportunity to obtain employment. We are growing together. We have a broader vision of what secular knowledge can bring us. I had to fight for my education. I want to make it possible for others to have these privileges."

Miriam was a modest, but outstanding, returned missionary in the Philippines, forced by circumstances to provide for her family. Inspired by the initial PEF fireside, she planned a career in Web design, but she soon found a good job in a travel agency that enabled her to continue with support for her family, attend school, and teach a class at the the local institute of religion. Her work in the agency was so distinguished that her employer promoted her to office manager. Her goal was to repay her PEF loan before graduating.

When Paulo went to the hospital for treatment of an illness, he observed laboratory workers testing his blood sample. He said, "Mom, I would like to work here one day." Through a PEF loan he studied and trained to be a lab specialist and soon his city selected him to be a trainee in the city's laboratory. "Now I work in three laboratories, one for the city and two for private laboratories."

One young man went to the Church Employment Resource Center in his area where he learned how to prepare for an interview. Attending an interview for a fine consultant position, he put on a suit and tie for the occasion. He faced stiff competition for the job. The woman conducting the interviews asked him why he was dressed so well. He explained that his church had given him training at the employment center. Then she asked him about his educational background and goals. He told her about the PEF program that was helping him obtain a good education. He concluded: "She was impressed and gave me the job. I received three times the salary of my last job. Last month I won the prize of being the best company salesman in the country."

Marco explained: "I am studying to be an X-ray technician. My family is very poor. I study at great sacrifice, working during the day and going to school at night. I travel by bicycle, often in the rain. My bishop is always at my side to help me. I became excited about the equipment and I am learning. My mission helped me a lot. Now I want to help others."

Aquatint, a sister, reported: "I am studying law and doing my best. I report regularly to my institute director. He is happy that I am making all A's. Some of my friends have been concerned that they have to repay the loans if they borrow from PEF. They asked me why President Hinckley requires us to repay the loans. I answer: the priesthood directs the Church. If we do what they counsel we will have stability and faith in our lives. We will do best if we follow the priesthood."

Another young man said: "PEF money is sacred. The money should be used in wisdom. The Lord knows we need to help young people so the Church can grow. We should apply for a loan only if we need it, and if we borrow, we must pay it back."

In telling his story, Vanderlei exemplifies what we are accomplishing with PEF in action. Vanderlei is married to Rosalia and they have two sons. He has now graduated from an excellent technical school with a degree in occupational safety. After a fine mission, he returned home to face conditions of poverty. For eight years he visited the school he eventually attended, with no way of raising the money to attend. The only employment he could manage to obtain was digging ditches and sewers. Nevertheless, with faith, he married, started a family, and served as branch president, growing the branch from 18 to 110 active members. Finally he learned about PEF, through which he was able to enter school to become an occupational safety specialist. His school, impressed with his number one standing in his class and with his character, offered him the job of safety manager for the new 10,000 student campus they were building. In six months he reduced the accident rate by 80%. His salary has increased fourfold. He is now highly regarded as a member of the high council in his stake and is on his way to a fine career. Surely this is what the Lord had in mind when He inspired the prophet and his associates to establish PEF.

Motivations are not always as pure and focused as were Vanderlei's. One young man was late for school after attending seminary; but his teacher gave him a ride in his automobile, and he made it on time. As he and his teacher rode toward school, the young man thought to himself: "Wow! This is a great car. It even has air conditioning. I want a car like this." Then he realized: "If I am going to have one, I will have to qualify and specialize." He explained that this motivated him to graduate from high school and get into training for marketing with the help of PEF.

Another young man, Fabian, lost his father when he was young, but before his father died he motivated his son to study. "I felt I would never have another father to help me, but now I know I have my Father in Heaven to bless me. Also, when I joined the Church the members helped me. But I had no way to study until Heavenly Father inspired the prophet to start PEF. I can feel my Heavenly Father orienting me as my father did."

Although we approve over 90% of the loan applications sent with the endorsement of the institute directors and the affirmation of worthiness and commitment to repay the loans by the bishop and stake president of each applicant, we do look at each request carefully in the loan committee to see if the plan makes sense. If it doesn't, we return the application for further consideration. One young man reported that he applied for a loan to study martial arts, but his application was returned unapproved. In his own words he reported: "As I thought about what I needed for my business, I realized that more than martial arts, I needed computer programming, so I applied for a loan to study in that field and it was approved. This is just what we needed in our business. There is a reason for everything."

We try to guide our young people to study in fields that are in higher demand in their communities. Douglas, of El Salvador, is studying refrigeration engineering, one of the jobs in greatest demand in Central America. As a result he already has a reputation for being able to handle refrigeration problems and has many repair jobs to do for those that have heard about his ability. He will soon open his own shop.

Another example is Tomas from Honduras who has become a specialist in auto electronics. As a result of his growing ability and reputation, an auto shop owner in his community handed over his business to Tomas in return for a percentage of the on-going profits. Tomas is a faithful leader in his Church and community.

Marila, an exceptional student in high school, could not earn enough money to further her education until PEF came along. She is now in a three-year program in Peru's most prestigious technical school. She is one of only two women in the school and has achieved the best grades in her class. Her future is bright. She reports: "I am so very grateful. I am repaying the loan. I will not let the prophet down."

Most of the young people are seeking jobs in a field new to them. Some are, however, seeking to improve their skills and standing to qualify for promotion in their present jobs. For example, Alfonso of Mexico has improved his position in a major graphic design firm with promotions that doubled his former income. The night our team met him in his home he was very late. He had worked a 13-hour day but arrived home excited with an announcement for his wife: "My boss is interested in making me manager of my design department! They say my leadership skills are strong—the very skills I developed during my mission. I am so grateful to the Lord for His goodness!"

We could continue, but these few stories illustrate the results of the first three years of the operation of the Perpetual Education Fund. Yes, we have had some young people who have not succeeded in their courses of study, and some have dropped out, but the great majority are succeeding and growing as envisioned in President Hinckley's historic announcement. President Hinckley leads, but he is not alone in sustaining this effort. Our Church leaders and our brothers and sisters are as one in helping bring to fruition the vision that has so inspired us. We who have had the burden and the honor of putting flesh on the spirit of PEF have firm testimonies of its source.

CHAPTER ELEVEN

WE'RE ALL IN THIS TOGETHER

Many shall come from the east and west, and
shall sit down with Abraham, and Isaac,
and Jacob, in the kingdom of heaven.

MATTHEW 8:11

P RESIDENT HINCKLEY'S ANNOUNCEMENT that the Church was
establishing PEF and a new Church department to administer
it immediately captured the hearts and minds of the Latter-day
Saints. For that matter, the acceptance and applause was nearly
universal in and out of the Church. The Saints appeared to be
looking for a practical way to help our young people rise from
poverty, and they resonated to President Hinckley's identification
of education and training for young adults in their own countries.
The essence of the message is that we are all in this together, and
we can help each other if we have the will.

Church members resonated immediately to the concept as
simple and right. We did not see it as an about-face or a revolutionary idea. Shortly after the announcement, I was at the airport
in Ontario, California. Waiting shoulder to shoulder with me at
the baggage claim was a young, dark-haired bishop from Salem,

Utah. On meeting me, he commented: "The announcement of the PEF sent shudders through my body. And I thought, 'This is so simple, and so right.' I wondered to myself, 'Why haven't we thought about this a long time ago.' "

The issue of poverty and lack of opportunity is complex and important. But the issue, which PEF is designed to address, is what can be done to help those in circumstances of poverty? One view of what should be done is to let circumstances take their course, and eventually the natural economic forces will take care of the problem. In other words, do nothing and what will be will be. Another view, one that President Hinckley has obviously adopted, is embodied in these scriptural words: "Verily I say, men should be anxiously engaged in a good cause, and do many things of their own free will, and bring to pass much righteousness; For the power is in them, wherein they are agents unto themselves. And inasmuch as men do good they shall in nowise lose their reward. But he that doeth not anything until he is commanded, and receiveth a commandment with doubtful heart, and keepeth it with slothfulness, the same is damned" (D&C 58:27–29).

So, under the direction of the Prophet, and exercising by delegation the keys and authority vested in him, we have launched PEF. It had the promise of helping thousands of people rise out of poverty into better conditions for family life and leadership in communities and in the Church. It is already doing that. In a great measure this program answers the question of what our responsibilities are to help those in poverty rise above their circumstances. The answer is that we are our brothers' keepers. We can develop an attitude of esteem for every man and woman we meet, and our religion requires that we do what we can to lift them. Our responsibility is to do what we can, wherever we are and in whatever circumstances we find ourselves in, to bless others.

Evidence that PEF is more than a financial assistance program was found in the first batch of semiannual reports submitted in January 2003. Areas reported that they had seen a growing cooperation between the several divisions of Church organization. The program was having a catalytic effect. In order to make PEF work, all have to work together. Interest in pursuing education and skill training has spread among returned missionaries worldwide. They have heard the prophet and gratefully responded to his message. Many who have begun the application process have found, through the career training and budgeting aspect of PEF, other resources that have obviated the need for a PEF loan.

Another important effect of PEF has been to require participants to overcome the tendency to expect something for nothing. One of the best ways to teach self-reliance is by having participants analyze their resources and prepare for a loan that they must repay. In this respect, PEF has had a powerful and salutary effect on applicants and recipients. The program has opened their eyes and taught them to rely on themselves.

One of the guiding principles of the program is to teach participants the importance of training for a vocation and employment in areas where skills are in demand. PEF strongly encourages loan recipients to engage in practical pursuits. PEF is teaching the concept of working and earning while improving skills.

Another guiding principle for the PEF team has been to ensure that the program provides a sound way to help people out of poverty and disadvantage without making them dependent. In the process, we have had the advantage of complete confidence in the concepts President Hinckley relayed to us and to the whole Church. It was typical of our prophet to share his innermost concerns with the membership, together with his suggested solutions to the problems that concerned him.

Clearly there are many less-advantaged people who are ambitious and desperately need to find a way to gain training, education, and jobs. We are not saying: "Let them fend for themselves; we can do nothing for them." Help is available.

As we come to a conclusion, we return to where we started and summarize the key principles involved in PEF. During an early evening on 31 March 2001, President Gordon B. Hinckley took his seat after addressing the worldwide gathering of men and boys in general priesthood meeting. He had startled and captivated the vast gathering by announcing that the Church would create a Perpetual Education Fund and a department to launch the associated program. His simple and powerful words had electrified all who heard them, and his closing testimony still echoed in their minds and hearts.

Hushed silence followed his words, and then a buzz started quietly and became more and more discernible. Some sat in tears, unable to speak. Others shared with those next to them: "We have heard a new revelation that will greatly impact this Church." Still others thought and some said: "This is so simple, and so right! Why haven't we thought of it before?" With voice and heart knitted together as one, the congregation echoed its "amen" as he concluded his historic address.

The prophet's words impacted virtually every Latter-day Saint in every country. Accustomed to praying for the poor and needy of the world, they now realized that a way had been opened to do something about supplying their needs by sharing what they had for that very purpose. In the days and months that followed, hundreds of thousands opened their purses and sent what they could to the fund in addition to their tithing and fast offerings. Almost all of us were moved to action of one kind or another. Many yearned to do more and offers to spend time helping create the program poured in from many sources. The fund grew, almost overnight, to major proportions. "It is a miracle," President Hinckley exclaimed over and over.

Following the announcement and explanation of the program of action, the Church established the new department to create the machinery necessary to make PEF a reality in the lives of the young adults it was designed to bless. Leaders were trained in their new and complex duties. Applications and procedures were perfected. The PEF board of directors examined and approved plans. The prophet assigned institutes of religion to launch the program in the field. This new assignment required these institutes to learn how to help their students make career choices, choose schools, and establish a personal budget. All of this required leaders to also undergo new training. Once the program was launched, students began the pursuit of the education, knowledge, and skills that would be marketable in their own countries. All of this led to increased enrollment in schools, completion of training, and finding employment. In due course this tremendous effort would lead to more successful and enriched family life. With the initiative underway, Church members awaited results. They have not been disappointed.

A young returned missionary in Mexico reported: "In

December 2001, I returned home after a full-time mission in the Mexico Vera Cruz Mission. My goals were high, but it appeared that I would be unable to achieve them due to finances, even with the help of my family. It was then that I discovered through PEF, my dream could perhaps be achieved.

"Immediately, I requested an interview with my priesthood leaders and four weeks later received notice of approval of a PEF loan that would help pay for my courses. Only last week I finished my studies and was immediately hired by a prestigious school to teach languages. They hired me at a salary three times greater than that which I was earning before. I can now begin my family. I was married on 20 December 2002. It is my desire that other young men such as I might be able to receive the benefits of this program. For this reason, I will do my best to return the amount of the loan as soon as possible."

The stories multiplied. The PEF has turned on the lights for many young adults and their families who have dwelt in the darkness of economic despair. We have identified some bright rays of light illuminating the lives of our young people. These stories are representative of many more, and new stories continue to unfold. Truly, PEF *is* a bright ray of hope.

Hope

Paul lists hope together with faith and charity as three qualities that must abide in disciples of Christ. To hope is to cherish a desire with anticipation or expectation of obtainment or fulfillment. We think of it in gospel terms as the expectation that though we die, we will yet live again and be saved with our Father in Heaven.

Our faithful young people cherish the hope of immortality and eternal life. It is hard, however, for them to become excited about the next life if they cannot anticipate having a good life while on earth, including an honorable career and full development of their skills and talents. When these goals appear impossible, their hope turns to hopelessness. Without such temporal hope the spiritual hope of salvation can seem unreal. Ideally, the gospel makes possible both kinds of hope.

PEF has already increased hope in young men and women all over the world. Just to know that their prophet is deeply concerned about them and wants the best for them has been a potent force in fostering hope, whether or not they needed or received a loan. To know that he has declared unequivocally that learning is the key to opportunity has turned their hearts and minds to education, training, and a search for a decent career. To know that career training, guidance, and, if necessary, a loan are available is powerful medicine. This reaching out to the youth may yet prove the most important principle and brightest light of PEF. It has kindled the light of hope nearly universally. Surely our Savior is pleased with the powerful spread of hope.

Self-Reliance

In all of his public references to PEF, President Hinckley has stressed the absolute need for self-reliance. These young people are not being given anything but an opportunity. "They will repay their loans to make it possible for others to be blessed as they have been blessed," President Hinckley declared without reservation. In one of our last board meetings he prophesied that almost every one of the young people would repay their loans. He believes in them and they are responding. The early returns on repayment rates by those receiving the first loans are encouraging. The more completely we have serviced the loans, the better we find the payment rate. We are still learning how to service the loans more effectively, and bishops and CES leaders are still learning how better to sustain the students in their training. Our interviews with the students evince a clear intent to repay their loans, and we intend to continue our efforts of loans servicing until we are certain that we have simplified the process, making it easy to make the payments. Perfecting loan servicing is our major goal for the year 2004.

Of course, as Emerson observed: "Self-reliance, the height and perfection of man, is reliance on God."[1] Those who attain self-reliance and learn to honor covenants have grown as God has desired them to grow. Loan recipients promise—solemnly covenant—to repay the loans to benefit others. Applicants for loans also promise to borrow only the amount absolutely necessary to help achieve their goals. They must pay all of their own room and board, stay in their own communities, and find ways to pay as much of their own school expenses as possible.

One young married couple applied for a PEF loan, taking the short training course designed to help them choose a career and budget their money. On reflection, and after reviewing their budget, they decided on nonessential expenditures they could reduce or eliminate, such as eating in fast-food establishments. They were startled to discover that by exercising frugality they did not even need a loan. They could pay for their own schooling.

PEF has already proven itself a catalyst to teach self-reliance to our Church members, particularly our young adults. What a benefit to them this will be! And the benefits will extend to their children, their wards and branches, and to the Church. Every community will be better as our people learn, practice, and exemplify self-reliance. Their self-esteem and confidence will soar and the effect will be miraculous. Church leaders have talked constantly about self-reliance. We have treated the subject in stake and general conferences, urging the Saints to practice it in their lives. Although such teachings have helped, we have needed something more. PEF may be that powerful and practical vehicle needed to instill self-reliance in the formative years of our young adults.

Sacrifice

We all understand that "sacrifice brings forth the blessings of heaven" (*Hymns,* no. 27). Inside of every one of us is something fine and wonderful, waiting for a chance to express itself— the urge to give up something of ours to bless the lives of our less fortunate brothers and sisters. PEF has provided a way to act on that noble impulse, and the Saints have responded by opening their hearts in a powerful manifestation of their willingness to sacrifice.

From the wards and branches have come literally millions of dollars. By far the greatest number of contributions have come from the rank-and-file members of the Church. Every day, every week, small contributions arrive to build the fund. If there were no other result than this outpouring of love and sacrifice, we would have to conclude that the fund had been a blessing to the Saints.

Loan recipients, too, make great sacrifices in the process, not only when they repay PEF loans, but also when they budget and eliminate nonessential activities in order to finance their training and schooling.

There is a corollary principle to the sacrifice involved here. It is the principle of making choices. When we see people suffering poverty and hopelessness, we want to reach out and balance the scales. A voice inside asks: "When we have so much, how can we rest without helping?" We enjoy fine clothing, beautiful homes, and expensive automobiles, but deep inside we know we must share with people who have nothing.

Leaders

Interviewers often ask our Church leaders what problems the Church faces. Finding leaders to meet the needs of the burgeoning Church ranks high on the list. Where will we find those leaders? They will come from good families. They always have and always will. But how can we develop stable families from which those leaders will come? This question is particularly pertinent in places like Latin America and the Philippines where our major growth is taking place. We will either solve that problem or find ourselves awash in a huge mass of leaderless members.

One of the best resources in the task of building families is PEF. With the help of its process of career guidance, budgeting, finding resources, and loans, as well as its emphasis on matching members and their skills with those skills needed in their communities, our young people are enabled to marry and raise families. With a little vision and financial help here and there, most of our young people can acquire needed training and find the resources to raise families. With good employment, they can also find the time to serve in the Church and in their communities. These wonderful things don't happen automatically. We have to pay attention to our youth, recognize their potential, and give them a boost. They will in turn help those who come after them, both by example and by replenishing the loan fund.

We will find leaders and excellent fathers and mothers coming out of this program. They will know how to build families based on gospel principles. This aspect of PEF may yet be the most important benefit of all.

Since its announcement, the Perpetual Education Fund has advanced from a vision painted by a prophet to a powerful reality. Great leaders will emerge from the work of this fund. PEF has shined a bright ray of hope on the path to education and training and independence. Church members have become more generous as they have sacrificed to help those needing help, and in the process are gaining spiritual blessings themselves.

President Hinckley has invited us to become a part of this bold initiative. Within the grasp of almost all Latter-day Saints is the ability to give something regularly to this fund and to other worthy endeavors.

This invitation helps those who contribute to PEF as well as those who improve themselves, to draw closer to our Savior. And both those who contribute and those who gain skills assist in the development of desperately needed Church leaders. Because of the principle of self-reliance, which is one of the foundational principles on which the Perpetual Education Fund is built, lifting up the less-advantaged will be done in the Lord's way, fostering hope and building character. It has been a joy and a privilege to have been involved in something that will bless in so many ways generations to come.

NOTE

1. Ralph Waldo Emerson, *The Complete Writings of Ralph Waldo Emerson* (New York: Wm. H. Wise & Co., 1929), 1165.

INDEX